The Arctic

the northern

William Scoresby

Alpha Editions

This edition published in 2024

ISBN : 9789367245095

Design and Setting By
Alpha Editions
www.alphaedis.com
Email - info@alphaedis.com

As per information held with us this book is in Public Domain. This book is a reproduction of an important historical work. Alpha Editions uses the best technology to reproduce historical work in the same manner it was first published to preserve its original nature. Any marks or number seen are left intentionally to preserve its true form.

Contents

PREFACE. .... - 1 -
CHAPTER I. .... - 2 -
CHAPTER II. .... - 13 -
CHAPTER III. .... - 27 -
CHAPTER IV. .... - 44 -
CHAPTER V. .... - 65 -
CHAPTER VI. .... - 89 -

PREFACE.

The following pages contain, in an abridged and somewhat modified form, the substance of the first volume of captain (now the rev. Dr.) Scoresby's work on the Arctic Regions and the Whale-fishery, Edinburgh, 1820; with the omission of the third chapter on the Hydrographical Survey of the Greenland Sea. It is now issued by the kind permission of the author; and a wider circulation may thus be secured for the interesting contents of his volumes than they could receive in their original and more costly form. Some few materials have also been collated from the valuable papers by the same author contributed to the "Edinburgh Philosophical Journal."

CHAPTER I.

REMARKS ON THE CELEBRATED QUESTION OF THE EXISTENCE OF A SEA COMMUNICATION BETWEEN THE ATLANTIC AND PACIFIC OCEANS, BY THE NORTH; WITH AN ACCOUNT OF THE PROGRESS OF DISCOVERY IN THE NORTHERN REGIONS.

The question of the existence of a navigable communication between the European and the Chinese seas, by the north, is one which has been long in agitation without being resolved, and has been often revived, with the most sanguine expectations of success, to be again abandoned as hopeless. The first attempts to reach China by sea, were made by steering along the coast of Africa toward the south, and the next, by proceeding from the European shore in a westerly direction. The former, which first proved successful, was accomplished by Vasquez de Gama, a Portuguese, in the year 1497-8; and the latter was undertaken by the renowned navigator, Columbus, in 1492. The notion of steering to India by the north-west, as the shortest way, was suggested about the middle or latter end of the fifteenth century, by John Vaz Costa Cortereal, who performed a voyage to Newfoundland about the year 1463-4; or, according to a more general opinion, by John Cabot, the father of the celebrated Sebastian Cabot, who attempted the navigation in 1497, and perhaps also in 1494-5. The idea of a passage to India by the North Pole was suggested by Robert Thorne, merchant of Bristol, as early as the year 1527; and the opinion of a passage by the north-east was proposed soon afterwards.

The universal interest which has been attached to this question of a sea communication between the Atlantic and Pacific Oceans, by the north, ever since it was first suggested, about three hundred and thirty or three hundred and fifty years ago, is fully proved by the facts, that the speculation has never but once been abandoned by the nations of Europe for more than twenty-five years together, and that there have been only three or four intervals of more than fifteen years in which no expedition was sent out in search of one or other of the supposed passages, from the year 1500 down to the present time. And it is not a little surprising that, after nearly a hundred different voyages have been undertaken with a view of discovering the desired communication with the Indian seas, all of which have failed, Britain should again revive and attempt the solution of this interesting problem.

Several facts may be brought forward, on which arguments of no mean force may be founded, in support of the opinion of the existence of a sea communication by the north between Europe and China. They may be enumerated in order.

1. The prevailing current in the Spitzbergen sea flows, we are well assured, during nine months of the year, if not all the year round, from the north-east towards the south-west. The velocity of this current may be from five to twenty miles per day, varying in different situations, but is most considerable near the coast of Old Greenland. The current, on the other hand, in the middle of Behring's Strait, as observed by lieutenant Kotzebue, sets strongly to the north-east, with a velocity, as he thought, of two miles and a half an hour; which is greater, however, by one-half than the rate observed by captain Cook.

2. By the action of the south-westerly current, a vast quantity of ice is annually brought from the north and east, and conducted along the east shore of Old Greenland as far as Cape Farewell, where such masses as still remain undissolved are soon destroyed by the influence of the solar heat and the force of the sea, to which they then become exposed from almost every quarter. This ice being entirely free from salt, and very compact, appears originally to have consisted of field-ice, a kind which perhaps requires the action of frost for many years to bring it to the thickness which it assumes. The quantity of heavy ice, in surface, which is thus annually dissolved, may, at a rough calculation, be stated to be about twenty thousand square leagues, while the quantity annually generated in the regions accessible to the whale-fishers is, probably, not more than one-fourth of that area. As such, the ice, which is so inexhaustible, must require an immense surface of sea for its generation, perhaps the whole or greater part of the so-called "Polar Basin;" the supply required for replacing what is dissolved in Behring's Strait, where the current sets towards the north, being, probably, of small moment. The current, in opposite parts of the northern hemisphere, being thus found to follow the same line of direction, indicates a communication between the two across the Poles; and the inexhaustible supply of ice, affording about fifteen thousand square leagues, to be annually dissolved above the quantity generated in the known parts of the Spitzbergen seas, supports the same conclusion.

3. The origin of the considerable quantity of drift-wood, found in almost every part of the Greenland sea, is traced to some country beyond the Pole, and may be brought forward in aid of the opinion of the existence of a sea communication between the Atlantic and the Pacific; which argument receives additional strength from the circumstance of some of the drift-wood being worm-eaten. This last fact I first observed on the shores of the island of Jan Mayen, in August, 1817, and confirmed it by more particular observation when at Spitzbergen the year following. Having no axe with me when I observed the worm-eaten wood, and having no means of bringing it away, I could not ascertain whether the holes observed in the timber were the work of a *ptinus* or a *pholas*. In either case, however, as it is not known

that these animals ever pierce wood in arctic countries, it is presumed that the worm-eaten drift-wood is derived from a transpolar region. Numerous facts of this nature might be adduced, all of which support the same conclusion.

4. The northern faces of the continents of Europe and Asia, as well as of that of America, so far as yet known, are such as renders it difficult even to imagine such a position for the unascertained regions, as to cut off the communication between the Frozen Sea, near the meridian of London, and that in the opposite part of the northern hemisphere, near Behring's Strait.

5. Whales, which have been harpooned in the Greenland seas, have been found in the Pacific Ocean; and whales, with stone lances sticking in their fat, (a kind of weapon used by no nation now known,) have been caught both in the sea of Spitsbergen and in Davis's Strait. This fact, which is sufficiently authenticated, seems to me the most satisfactory argument.

The Russians, it appears, have, at intervals, discovered all the navigation between Archangel and the Strait of Behring, excepting a portion of about two hundred miles, occupied by the eastern part of a noss, or promontory, lying between the rivers Khatanga and Piacina. The northern extremity of this noss, called Cape Ceverovostochnoi, appears to have been doubled by lieutenant Prontschitscheff, in the year 1735, so that ice, and perhaps some small islands, seem in this place to form the great obstruction to the navigation. As far as can be well substantiated, the portion of the route between Archangel and Kamtchatka, which has been hitherto accomplished, clearly proves that, if a sea communication between the Atlantic and Pacific by the north-east really exists, it could never be practicable in one year. Inasmuch as the Russians were five or six years in performing so much of the navigation as has been accomplished, though they employed a number of different vessels in the undertaking, it is probable that the voyage could never be performed in one vessel, unless by mere accident, in less than eight or ten years. It is clear, therefore, that the discovery of a "north-east passage" could never be of any advantage to our commerce with China or India.

Though, however, the voyages undertaken in search of a north-east passage by the different nations of Europe have amounted to about twelve, besides numerous partial attempts by the Russians, and though all of them have failed in their principal intention, yet they have not been wholly lost to us; the Spitzbergen whale and seal fisheries, so valuable to the country, with the trade to Archangel, having arisen out of them.

The voyages of Davis, in the years 1585-6 and 1587-8, of Hudson, in 1610, and of Baffin, in 1616, were the source of the greatest part of the discoveries which have been made in the countries situated to the northward and westward of the south point of Greenland. To these regions, consisting of what have been called bays and straits, the names of these celebrated voyagers have been applied. All the voyages, indeed, since undertaken for discovery in the same quarter, amounting to nearly thirty, have done little more than confirm the researches of these three individuals, and show how little there was to be found, instead of discovering anything of moment. The ostensible object of most of these voyages, was the discovery of a shorter passage to India than that by the Cape of Good Hope, by the north-west. The existence of such a passage is not yet either proved or refuted. In an account of "a Voyage to Hudson's Bay," by Henry Ellis, such a passage is inferred to exist from the following considerations:—the want of trees on the west side of Hudson's Bay beyond a certain latitude; the appearance of a certain ridge of mountains lying near the same coast, and extending in a direction parallel to it; the direct testimony of the Indians, that they have seen the sea beyond the mountains, and have observed vessels navigating therein; and, most particularly, the nature and peculiarities observed in the tides. This latter argument is by far the most conclusive. From observations on the winds and tides in the Baltic, Mediterranean, and other inland seas, Ellis proceeds to show, that every circumstance with regard to the tides in Hudson's Bay is different from what would take place in an inland sea, and then concludes that Hudson's Bay is not such a sea, but has some opening which communicates with the Frozen Ocean on the north-west.

Other arguments, which have been offered in favour of the separation of Greenland from America, are deduced from the existence of a current setting from the north—from the circumstance of icebergs and drift-wood being brought down by the current—from whales wounded in the Spitzbergen seas having been caught in Davis's Strait—from the position of the land, as represented on skins by the native American Indians—and from the occurrence of certain plants in Greenland, which are natives of Europe, but have never been found in any part of the American continent.

The opinion appears to be quite incorrect, that if a passage were discovered, it would, probably, be open above half the year. I imagine it would be only at intervals of years that it would be open at all, and then, perhaps, for no longer time than eight or ten weeks in a season. Hence, as affording a navigation to the Pacific Ocean, the discovery of a north-west passage would be of no service. For many reasons, however, the examination of these interesting countries is an object worthy of the attention of a great nation. The advantages that have already arisen to Britain from the voyages undertaken in search of a north-west passage are, the establishment of the Davis's Strait's whale-fishery, and of the trade of the Hudson's Bay company, so that the expenditure has not altogether been lost.

The adventurous spirit manifested by our early navigators, in performing such hazardous voyages in small barks, in which we should be scrupulous of trusting ourselves across the German Ocean, is calculated to strike us with surprise and admiration, while the correctness of their investigations gives us a high opinion of their perseverance and talent. The famous voyage of Baffin, in which the bay bearing his name was discovered, was performed in a vessel of only fifty-five tons' burden; that of Hudson, in which also the bay called by his name was first navigated, in the very same vessel; and the voyages of Davis chiefly in vessels of fifty, thirty-five, and ten tons' burden.

In perusing the voyages of our old navigators, it is particularly gratifying to those who consider religion as the chief business of this life, to observe the strain of piety and dependence upon Divine Providence which runs through almost every narrative. Their honest and laudable acknowledgments of a particular interference of the Almighty, working out deliverance for them in times of difficulty and danger, and their frequent declarations expressive of their reliance upon Providence, for assistance and protection in their adventurous undertakings, are worthy of our imitation. Thus, while our modern voyagers are much in the habit of attributing their most remarkable deliverances to "luck," "chance," and "fortune," those of old evidenced certainly a more Christian-like feeling, under such circumstances, by referring their deliverances to that great Being, from whom alone every good thing must be derived. They only who have a similar dependence on Providence, and who have been occasionally in trying situations, can duly appreciate the confidence and comfort which this belief is calculated to afford under the most appalling circumstances.

The class of vessels best adapted for discovery in the Polar seas, seems to be that of one hundred to two hundred tons' burden. They are stronger, more easily managed, in less danger of being stoved or crushed by ice, and not so expensive as those of larger dimensions. An increase of size is a diminution of comparative strength; and hence it is evident, that a vessel intended for discovery should be just large enough for conveying the requisite stores and provisions, and for affording comfortable accommodation to the navigators, but no larger. Perhaps a vessel about one hundred and fifty tons' burden would be fully sufficient to answer every purpose. The navigation of the Polar seas, which is peculiar, requires in a particular manner an extensive knowledge of the nature, properties, and usual motions of the ice, and it can only be performed to the best advantage by those who have had long experience in working a ship in icy situations. It might be a material assistance to those employed in completing the examination of Baffin's Bay, as well as productive of some interesting information in meteorological phenomena, were a vessel or two to remain in the northern part of this bay through the winter. There is very little doubt that the vessel would, by this method, be released by the ice as early as May or June, and thus be afforded about double the time of research that could be obtained by wintering out of the bay. There would not, I imagine, be any very great danger in making this experiment, provided a sufficient quantity of fresh provisions, for the prevention of the scurvy among the crew, were taken out, and certain precautions adopted for the preservation of the ships. The ingenious apparatus invented by Mr. Thomas Morton designed to supersede, in repairing vessels, the necessity of dry docks, might be eminently advantageous.

In seas perpetually encumbered with ice, and probably crowded with islands, if not divided by necks of land, the chance of great discoveries and of extensive navigations towards the north-west, even under the best arrangements and under the boldest seamen, is but small. The most certain method of ascertaining the existence of a communication between the Atlantic and Pacific, along the northern face of America, would doubtless be by journeys on land. Men there are who, being long used to travel upon snow in the service of the Hudson's Bay company, would readily undertake the journey by the interior lakes of North America to the Frozen Ocean, or, in case of a continuity of land being found, to the very Pole itself, of whose success we should certainly have a reasonable ground of hope. The practicability of this mode of making discoveries has been fully proved by the expeditions of Mackenzie and Hearne; and a possibility of performing very long journeys on snow can be attested, from personal experience, by those who have wintered a few times in Hudson's Bay.

The plan of performing a journey in this way, for discovering the northern termination of the American continent, and for tracing it round to its junction with the coasts of the same country, washed by the Atlantic, might be in some measure as follows. The party intended for this expedition, which should consist of as few individuals as possible, ought, perhaps, in the course of one summer, to make their way to one of the interior settlements of the Hudson's Bay company, or of the Canadian traders, such as Slave Fort, on the great Slave Lake, situated in the 62nd degree of latitude, or Fort Chepewyan, near the Athapescow Lake, in latitude 58° 40', from whence sir Alexander Mackenzie embarked on his voyage to the Frozen Ocean, and there abide during the first winter. Supposing the travellers to winter at Slave Fort, they might calculate on being within the distance of two hundred leagues, or thirty or forty days' journey, moderate travelling, of the Frozen Ocean. In the month of March or April, the party, consisting of two or three Europeans, one or two Esquimaux interpreters, and two or more Indian guides, provided with everything requisite for the undertaking, might set out towards the north. On the arrival of the travellers among the Esquimaux, their Indian guides, from fear of this nation, would probably desert them, but the presence of their Esquimaux interpreters would secure them a good reception. When once they should meet with this people, they would have a strong evidence of being near the sea, as it is well known the Esquimaux never retire far from the coast. On their arrival at the coast, it will be necessary to associate with the Esquimaux, to submit in some measure to their mode of living, and, to effect any considerable discovery, it might be requisite to spend a winter or two among them, in which case they might trace the line of the Frozen Ocean to such a length, that the place where it joins the western coast of Baffin's Bay, or Hudson's Bay, or the eastern side of Greenland, would be determined. Or, if it should be objectionable to winter among the Esquimaux, several expeditions might be sent out at the same time from different stations, and on different meridians. The expense of three or four such expeditions over land would probably be less than that of one expedition by sea.

The scheme suggested by Robert Thorne, of Bristol, of finding a passage to India across the North Pole, about the year 1527, appears to have been immediately attempted by an expedition, consisting of two ships, sent out by order of Henry VIII.; one of the ships, we are informed, was lost; of the nature of the success of the other we have but a very unsatisfactory account. After this voyage, Barentz, Heemskerke, and Ryp, attempted the transpolar navigation, in 1596; Hudson, in 1607; Jonas Poole, in 1610 and 1611; Baffin and Fotherby, in 1614; Fotherby, in 1615; Phipps, in 1773; and Buchan and Franklin, in 1818. The highest latitude attained by any of these navigators did not, it would appear, exceed 81°. My father, in the ship Resolution, of Whitby, in the year 1806, with whom I then served as chief mate, sailed to a much higher latitude. Our latitude, on three occasions, in the month of May, as derived from observations taken with a sextant by myself and my father, was 80° 50' 28", 81° 1' 53", and 81° 12' 42"; after which we sailed so far to the northward as made it about 81° 30', which is one of the closest approximations to the Pole which I conceive has been well authenticated.

Whatever may be our opinion of the accounts brought forward by some parties to prove the occasional accessibility of the 83rd or 84th parallel of north latitude, of this we may be assured, that the opinion of an open sea round the Pole is altogether chimerical. It is urged, indeed, that the extraordinary power of the sun, about the summer solstice, is so far greater at the Pole than at the Equator, as to destroy all the ice generated in the winter season, and to render the temperature of the Pole warmer and more congenial to feeling than it is in some places lying nearer the Equator. So far, however, from the actual influence of the sun, though acknowledged at a certain season to be greater at the Pole than at the Equator, being above what it is calculated to be by the ordinary formulæ for temperature, it is found by experiment in latitude 78° to be greatly below it—how then can the temperature of the Pole be expected to be so very different? From the remarks in the ensuing pages, it will be shown that ice is annually formed during nine months of the year in the Spitzbergen sea, and that neither calm weather, nor the proximity of land, is essential for its formation. Can it, then, be supposed, that at the Pole, where the mean temperature is probably as low as 10°, the sea is not full of ice? If the masses of ice, which usually prevent the advance of navigators beyond the 82nd degree of north latitude, be extended in a continued series to the Pole, (of which, unless there be land in the way, there appears no doubt,) the expectation of reaching the Pole by sea is altogether vain. By land, however, I do not conceive the journey would be impracticable. It would not exceed one thousand two hundred miles, (six hundred miles each way,) and might be performed on sledges, drawn by dogs or reindeer, or even on foot. Foot travellers would require to draw the apparatus and provisions, necessary for the undertaking, on sledges by hand, and in this way, with good dispatch, the journey would occupy at least two months; but, with the assistance of dogs, it might, probably, be accomplished in a little less time. With favourable winds, great advantage might be derived from sails set upon the sledges, which sails, when the travellers were at rest, would serve for the erection of tents. Small vacancies in the ice would not prevent the journey, as the sledges might be adapted so as to answer the purpose of boats, nor would the usual unevenness of the ice, nor the depth or softness of the snow, be an insurmountable difficulty, as journeys of nearly equal length, and under similar inconveniences, have been accomplished.

Among many similar accounts, there is one related by Muller, in his "Voyages from Asia to America," of a Cossack having actually performed a journey of about eight hundred miles in a sledge, drawn by dogs, across a surface of ice lying to the northward of the Russian dominions, which sufficiently establishes the practicability of a journey across the ice to the Pole. Alexei Markoff, a Cossack, was sent to explore the Frozen Ocean, in the summer of the year 1714, by order of the Russian government, but finding the sea so crowded with ice that he was unable to make any progress in discovery, he formed the design of travelling in sledges, during the winter or spring of the year, over the ice, which might then be expected to be firm and compact. Accordingly, he prepared several of the country sledges, drawn by dogs, and accompanied by eight persons, he set out on the 10th of March from the mouth of the Jana, in latitude 70° 30', and longitude about 138° east. He proceeded for seven days northward, as fast as his dogs could draw, which, under favourable circumstances, is eighty or one hundred versts a day, until his progress was impeded, about the 78th degree of latitude, by the ice elevated into prodigious mountains. This prevented his further advance; at the same time, falling short of provisions for his dogs, his return was effected with difficulty; several of his dogs died for want, and were given to the rest for their support. On the 3rd of April, he arrived at Ust-Jauskoe Simowie, the place from whence he started, after an absence of twenty-four days, during which time he appears to have travelled about eight hundred miles. The journey of Markoff was nearly equal in extent to the projected journey to the Pole, and there appears no very great reason why a person equally adventurous with Markoff, and better provided, might not in a similar manner reach the Pole.

The first considerable discovery which appears to have been made in or near the arctic circle, was the result of accident; one of the numerous Scandinavian depredators, who, in the ninth century, cruised the northern seas in search of plunder, having been driven, by a long-continued storm, from the eastward upon the coast of Iceland, in the year 861. This island, from the quantity of snow seen on the mountains, was, by its discoverer Naddodd, at first called *Schnee*, or *Snowland*. It was visited by a Swede of the name of Gardar Suaffarson, three years after its discovery, and afterwards by another Swede, Flocke, from whom it received the name of *Iceland*. It was again visited in the year 874, by Ingolf and Lief, two Norwegians, and became the seat of a Norwegian colony.

The coast of Norway, to the entrance of the White Sea, was examined about this period by a person of the name of Ohthere, a Norwegian, who himself gave an account of his voyage to Alfred the Great, by whom it has been handed down to us along with the translation of the Ormesta of Orosius.

About the middle, or towards the end of the tenth century, an extensive country, to the westward of Iceland, was discovered by one of the colonists of the name of Gunbiorn, which country was visited, in the year 982, by one Eric Rauda, who had fled from Norway to Iceland, to avoid the punishment due to the crime of murder and various other offences. To this country he gave the name of *Greenland*, and in consequence of his exaggerated account of its products and appearance, a respectable colony was founded. About the year 1001, one of the Iceland colonists, Biorn by name, was accidentally driven by a storm to the southward of Greenland, where he discovered a new country, covered with wood. Lief, the son of Eric Rauda, fitted out a vessel, and visited the country. Grapes were discovered in it, and from this circumstance it was called *Vinland*; the day was eight hours long in winter, whence it appears that it must have been somewhere on the coast of North America, probably on the shore of Newfoundland.

The Christian religion was introduced into Iceland and Greenland about the year 1000, and within a hundred years afterwards generally diffused. Above sixteen churches were then built, and two convents. These buildings, as well as the habitations of the colonists, were erected near the southern point of Greenland. They had two settlements, the most western of which increased up to four parishes, containing one hundred farms or villages; and the most eastern, to twelve parishes, one hundred and ninety villages, one bishop's see, and two convents. The intercourse between Greenland and the rest of the world was intercepted about the year 1406, when the seventeenth bishop attempted to reach his see, but was prevented by ice. Since the beginning of the fifteenth century, these unfortunate colonists have been of necessity left to themselves, and not having been heard of, are supposed to have perished; but whether they were destroyed by their enemies the Esquimaux, or perished for want of their usual supplies, or were carried off by a destructive pestilence, as some have imagined, is still matter of doubt. Various attempts have been made by order of the Danish government for recovery of this country, and to ascertain the fate of these colonists, but hitherto without success.

Alter the voyages of Columbus, a new stimulus was offered to the enterprising trader, and to those who might be desirous of prosecuting the task of discovery, and a Portuguese navigator, John Vaz Costa Cortereal, about the year 1463 or 1464, tried the passage to India by the west, on a parallel far to the northward of that pursued by Columbus. In this voyage the land of Newfoundland appears to have been seen. The same voyage was attempted by Sebastian Cabot, a Venetian, in the year 1497, and by Gaspar Cortereal and Michael Cortereal, sons of the previously named Costa. Both these brothers perished, and a third brother, who would have followed in search of them, was prohibited from embarking by the king of Portugal.

An important voyage of discovery was that of sir Hugh Willoughby, in the year 1553, in which the coast now called Nova Zembla was discovered, and the Russian territory on the east side of the White Sea. In consequence of this expedition, a regular trade was established with Russia, which was accomplished under various privileges. In the year 1556, further discoveries in the same quarter were made by Stephen Burrough. Then followed the voyages of Martin Frobisher and John Davis; the latter in the year 1585. He proceeded along the west side of Greenland, and then crossing an open sea to the north-westward, discovered land in latitude 66° 40', giving names to the different parts of the coast which has since been denominated *Cumberland Island*. In the course of this voyage, they met with a multitude of natives, whom they found a very tractable people, and liberal in their mode of trafficking. In the following year, Davis prosecuted another voyage, but with no discovery of any consequence; and again also, for the third time, in the year following.

Amongst several expeditions sent out by the Dutch, to explore a passage to India and China by the north-east, that of two ships, under the pilotage of William Barentz, is the most memorable. It sailed from Amsterdam the 10th of May, 1596. After having discovered Spitzbergen, the two ships pursued different courses, and Barentz, while endeavouring to sail round Nova Zembla, became entangled in the ice. They were, in consequence, compelled to winter in this desolate and frozen country. "The journal of the proceedings of these poor people," as Mr. Barrow beautifully observes, "during this cold, comfortless, dark, and dreadful winter is intensely and painfully interesting. No murmuring escapes them in their hopeless and afflicted situation; but such a spirit of true piety, and a tone of such mild and subdued resignation to Divine Providence, breathe throughout the whole narrative, that it is impossible to peruse the simple tale of their sufferings, and contemplate their forlorn situation, without the deepest emotion." Forcibly, indeed, does their narrative illustrate the mind's independence of external comforts, and the peace and joy to be derived from trust in God, and cordial submission to his appointments. Part of the sufferers made their escape in two open boats from this dismal country, in the following summer, and after a perilous and painful voyage, of above one thousand one hundred miles, arrived in safety at Cola; but Barentz, with some others, was overcome by the severity of the climate, and the extraordinary exertions which he was obliged to make, and died.

In the year 1608, Henry Hudson was employed in search of a north-east passage; and, in 1610, in a voyage of discovery towards the north-west, in a vessel of fifty-five tons' burden. It was on this occasion that he discovered the bay which bears his name, hauled his ship on shore in a convenient situation, and wintered there. They fell short of provisions, and the following summer the crew mutinied, and abandoned their captain, his son, and others of the crew, to a most cruel fate. In 1616 was accomplished the remarkable voyage of William Baffin, attended by discoveries of a most extensive nature in the bay which bears his name, which, though regarded with considerable doubt at first, have since been abundantly confirmed by the labours of captain Ross and lieutenant Parry.

In March, 1822, the ship Baffin sailed from Liverpool, and reached 80° north latitude without experiencing any frost; on the 27th April, we arrived within ten miles of Spitzbergen, and were stopped in latitude 80° 30' by main ice. Afterwards, we encountered a most heavy gale, the thermometer falling in the space of sixteen hours 34°, being the most remarkable change I ever experienced in Greenland seas. On the 1st May, we advanced to only five hundred and sixty-six miles' distance from the Pole, and subsequently discovered the eastern coast of Greenland, a continuation towards the north of the coast on which the ancient Icelandic colonies were planted. We surveyed and named various parts of this coast, to the extent of about eight hundred miles, and found traces of inhabitants. It was inferred that Greenland is probably a great group of islands. The expedition returned on the 18th September, in the same year.

CHAPTER II.

DESCRIPTIVE ACCOUNT OF SOME OF THE POLAR COUNTRIES.

Spitzbergen extends furthest towards the north of any country yet discovered. It is surrounded by the Arctic Ocean, or Greenland Sea; and, though the occasional resort of persons drawn thither for purposes of hunting and fishing, does not appear to have been ever inhabited. It lies between the latitudes 76° 30' and 80° 7' north, and between the longitude of 9°, and, perhaps, 22° east; but some of the neighbouring islands extend at least as far north as 80° 40', and still further towards the east than the mainland of Spitzbergen. The western part of this country was discovered by Barentz, Heemskerke, and Ryp, in two vessels, fitted out of Amsterdam, on the 19th of June, 1596, who, from the numerous peaks and acute mountains observed on the coast, gave it the appropriate name of Spitzbergen, signifying "sharp mountains." It was afterwards named *Newland*, or *King James's Newland*, and then *Greenland*, being supposed to be a continuation towards the east of the country so-called by the Icelanders. It was re-discovered by Henry Hudson, an English navigator, in 1607, and four years afterwards became the resort of the English for the purpose of taking whales, since which period its shores have annually been visited by one or other of the nations of Europe, with the same object, to the present time. And though the soil of the whole of this remote country does not produce vegetables suitable or sufficient for the nourishment of a single human being, yet its coasts and adjacent seas have afforded riches and independence to thousands.

This country exhibits many interesting views, with numerous examples of the sublime. Its stupendous hills, rising by steep acclivities from the very margin of the ocean to an immense height; its surface, contrasting the native, protruding, dark-coloured rocks, with the burden of purest snow and magnificent ices, altogether constitute an extraordinary and beautiful picture.

The whole of the western coast is mountainous and picturesque, and though it is shone upon by a four months' sun every year, its snowy covering is never wholly dissolved, nor are its icy monuments of the dominion of frost ever removed. The valleys, opening towards the coast, and terminating in the background with a transverse chain of mountains, are chiefly filled with everlasting ice. The inland valleys, at all seasons, present a smooth and continued bed of snow, in some places divided by considerable rivulets, but in others exhibiting a pure unbroken surface for many leagues in extent. Along the western coast, the mountains take their rise from within a league of the sea, and some from its very edge. Few tracts of table-land, of more than a league in breadth, are to be seen, and in many places the blunt termination of mountain ridges project beyond the regular line of the coast, and overhang the waters of the ocean. The southern part of Spitzbergen consists of groups of insulated mountains, little disposed in chains, or in any determinate order, having conical, pyramidal, or ridged summits, sometimes round-backed, frequently terminating in points, and occasionally in acute peaks, not unlike spires. An arm of a short mountain chain, however, forms the southern cape, or Point Look-out, but a low flat, in the form of a fish's tail, of about forty square miles in surface, constitutes the termination of the coast. Other promontories, lying nearly north and south, are of a similar nature.

To the northward of Charles's Island the mountains are more dispersed in chains than they are to the southward. The principal ridge lies nearly north and south, and the principal valley extends from the head of Cross Bay to the northern face of the country, a distance of forty or fifty miles. An inferior chain of hills, two or three leagues from the coast, runs parallel with the shore, from which lateral ridges project into the sea, and terminate in mural precipices. Between these lateral ridges, some of the largest icebergs on the coast occur. The most remarkable mountains I have seen are situated near Horn Sound, on Charles's Island, and near King's Bay. Horn Mount, or Hedge-hog Mount, so-called from an appearance of spires on the top, when seen in some positions, takes its rise from a small tract of alpine land, on the southern side of Horn Sound. It has different summits, chiefly in the form of spires, one of which is remarkably elevated. I had an opportunity of determining its height in the year 1815. From one set of observations its altitude came out 1,457 yards, and from another 1,473 yards, the mean of which is 1,465 yards, or 4,395 feet. Another peak, a few miles further to the northward, appeared to be 3,306 feet high.

On Charles's Island is a curious peak, which juts into the sea. It is crooked, perfectly naked, being equally destitute of snow and verdure, and from its black appearance, or pointed figure, has been denominated the Devil's Thumb. Its height may be about 1,500 or 2,000 feet. The middle hook of the foreland, as the central part of the chain of mountains in Charles's Island is called, is a very interesting part of the coast. These mountains, which are, perhaps, the highest land adjoining the sea which is to be met with, take their rise at the water's edge, and, by a continued ascent of an angle at first of about 30°, and increasing to about 45°, or more, each comes to a point, with the elevation of about six-sevenths of an English mile. This portion of the chain exhibits five distinct summits, some of them to appearance are within half a league, horizontal distance, of the margin of the sea. The points formed by the top of two or three of them are so fine, that the imagination is at a loss to conceive of a place on which an adventurer, attempting the hazardous exploit of climbing one of the summits, might rest. Were such an undertaking practicable, it is evident it could not be effected without imminent danger. Besides extraordinary courage and strength requisite in the adventurer, such an attempt would need the utmost powers of exertion, as well as the most irresistible perseverance. Frederick Martens, in his excellent account of a "Voyage to Spitzbergen," undertaken in the year 1671, describes some of the cliffs as consisting of but one stone from the bottom to the top, and as smelling very sweet where covered with lichens. In Magdalen Bay, the rocks he describes as lying in a semicircular form, having at each extremity two high mountains, with natural excavations, "after the fashion of a breastwork," and, at their summits, points and cracks like battlements.

Some of the mountains of Spitzbergen are well-proportioned, four-sided pyramids, rising out of a base of a mile, or a mile and a half, to a league square; others form angular chains, resembling the roof of a house, which recede from the shore in parallel ridges, until they dwindle into obscurity in the distant perspective. Some exhibit the exact resemblance of art, but in a style of grandeur exceeding the famed pyramids of the east, or even the more wonderful tower of Babel. An instance of such a regular and magnificent work of nature is seen near the head of King's Bay, consisting of three piles of rocks, of a regular form, known by the name of the Three Crowns. They rest on the top of the ordinary mountains, each commencing with a square table, or horizontal stratum of rock, on the top of which is another of similar form and height, but of smaller area; this is continued by a third, a fourth, and so on, each succeeding stratum being less than the next below it, until it forms a pyramid of steps, almost as regular, to appearance, as if worked by art.

Many of the mountains of Spitzbergen are inaccessible. The steepness of the ascent, and the looseness of the rocks, with the numerous lodgments of ice in the cliffs, or on the sides of the cliffs, constitute in many places insurmountable obstacles. Some hills, indeed, may be climbed with tolerable safety, but generally the attempt is hazardous. Many have fallen and lost their lives, especially in the descent. When Barentz and Heemskerke discovered Cherie Island, on their advance towards the north, they also discovered Spitzbergen, when some daring fellows among their sailors, who had been collecting birds' eggs, climbed a high, steep mountain, resembling those of Spitzbergen, and unexpectedly found themselves in a most perilous situation, for, on turning to descend, the way by which they had advanced presented a dismal assemblage of pointed rocks, perpendicular precipices, and yawning chasms. The view of the danger of the ascent struck them with terror. No relief, however, could be afforded them, and they were bewildered among the rocks. At length, after a most anxious and painful exercise, in which they found it necessary to slide down the rocks, while lying flat on their bodies, they reached the foot of the cliff in safety. Barentz, who had observed their conduct from the shore, gave them a sharp reproof for their temerity.

One of the most interesting appearances to be found in Spitzbergen, is the iceberg. These mountains of ice occur in the valleys adjoining the coast of Spitzbergen, and other Polar countries. A little to the northward of Charles's Island are the *Seven Icebergs*. Each of these occupies a deep valley, opening towards the sea, formed by hills of about two thousand feet elevation on the sides, and terminated in the interior by the chain of mountains, of perhaps three thousand to three thousand three hundred feet in height, which follows the line of the coast. They are exactly of the nature and appearance of glaciers, and there are many others of various sizes along the shores of this remarkable country.

It is not easy to form an adequate conception of these truly wonderful productions of nature. Their magnitude, their beauty, and the contrast they form with the gloomy rocks around, produce sensations of lively interest. Their upper surfaces are generally concave; the higher parts are always covered with snow, and have a beautiful appearance, but the lower parts, in the latter end of every summer, present a bare surface of ice. The front of each, which varies in height from the level of the ocean to four hundred or five hundred feet above it, lies parallel with the shore, and is generally washed by the sea. This part, resting on the strand, is undermined to such an extent by the sea, when any way turbulent, that immense masses, loosened by the freezing of water, lodged in the recesses in winter, or by the effect of streams of water running over its surface and through its chasms in summer, break asunder, and, with a thundering noise, fall into the sea.

On an excursion to one of the Seven Icebergs, in July, 1818, I was particularly successful in witnessing one of the grandest effects which these Polar glaciers ever present. A strong north-westerly swell having, for some hours, been beating on the shore, had loosened a number of fragments attached to the iceberg, and various heaps of broken ice denoted recent shoots of the seaward edge. As we rode towards it, with a view of proceeding close to its base, I observed a few little pieces fall from the top, and, while my eye was fixed on the place, an immense column, probably fifty feet square, and one hundred and fifty feet high, began to leave the parent ice at the top, and leaning majestically forward with an accelerated velocity, fell with an awful crash into the sea. The water into which it plunged was converted into an appearance of vapour, or smoke, like that from a furious cannonading. The noise was equal to that of thunder, which it nearly resembled. The column which fell was nearly square, and in magnitude resembled a church. It broke into thousands of pieces. This circumstance was a happy caution, for we might inadvertently have gone to the base of the icy cliff, from whence masses of considerable magnitude were continually breaking.

This iceberg was full of rents as high as any of our people ascended upon it, extending in a direction perpendicularly downward, and dividing it into innumerable columns. The surface was very uneven, being furrowed and cracked all over. This roughness appeared to be occasioned by the melting of the snow, some streams of water being seen running over the surface; and others, having worn away the superficial ice, could still be heard pursuing their course through subglacial channels to the front of the iceberg, where, in transparent streams, or in small cascades, they fell into the sea. In some places, chasms of several yards in width were seen, in others they were only a few inches or feet across. One of the sailors, who attempted to walk across the iceberg, imprudently stepped into a narrow chasm, filled up with snow to the general level. He instantly plunged up to his shoulders, and might, but for the sudden extension of his arms, have been buried in the gulf.

Icebergs are, probably, formed of more solid ice than glaciers, but, in every other respect, they are very similar. The ice of which they consist is, indeed, a little porous, but considerable pieces are found of perfect transparency. Being wholly produced from rain or snow, the water is necessarily potable. Icebergs have, probably, the same kind of origin as glaciers, and the time of their first stratum is nearly coeval with the land on which they are lodged. Though large portions may be frequently separated from the lower edge, or, by large avalanches from the mountain summit, be hurled into the sea, yet the annual growth replenishes the loss, and, probably, on the whole, produces a perpetual increase in thickness.

Spitzbergen and its islands, with some other countries within the Arctic Circle, exhibit a kind of scenery which is altogether novel. The principal objects which strike the eye are innumerable mountainous peaks, ridges, precipices, or needles, rising immediately out of the sea, to an elevation of three thousand or four thousand feet, the colour of which, at a moderate distance, appears to be blackish shades of brown, green, grey, and purple; snow or ice, in striæ, or patches, occupying the various clefts and hollows in the sides of the hills, capping some of the mountain summits, and filling with extended beds the most considerable valleys; and ice of the glacier-form occurring at intervals all along the coast in particular situations, as already described, in prodigious accumulations. The glistening, or vitreous appearance of the iceberg precipices, the purity, whiteness, and beauty of the sloping expanse, formed by the adjoining or intermixed mountains and rocks, perpetually "covered with a mourning veil of black lichens," with the sudden transitions into a robe of purest white, where patches or beds of snow occur, present a variety and extent of contrast altogether peculiar, which, when enlightened by the occasional ethereal brilliancy of the Polar sky, and harmonized in its serenity with the calmness of the ocean, constitute a picture both novel and magnificent. There is, indeed, a kind of majesty, not to be conveyed in words, in these extraordinary accumulations of snow and ice in the valleys, and in the rocks above rocks, and peaks above peaks, in the mountain groups, seen rising above the ordinary elevation of the clouds, and terminating occasionally in crests of everlasting snow, especially when you approach the shore under shelter of the impenetrable density of a summer fog, in which case the fog sometimes disperses like the drawing of a curtain, when the strong contrast of light and shade, brightened by a cloudless atmosphere and powerful sun, bursts on the senses in a brilliant exhibition. Here are to be beheld the glories of that one God, who is the Maker of all things in heaven and on earth, and who, unlike the false deities of heathen nations, is not confined in his presence and government to any particular zone of the earth's surface, but illustrates the skill and excellence of his creation, both in the beauties of icy and torrid climes.

A remarkable deception, in the apparent distance of the land, is to be attributed to the strong contrast of light and shade, and the great height and steepness of the mountains, displayed in these regions. Any strangers to the Arctic countries, however capable of judging of the distance of land generally, must be completely at a loss in their estimations when they approach within sight of Spitzbergen. When at the distance of twenty miles, it would be no difficult matter to induce even a judicious stranger to undertake a passage in a boat to the shore, from the belief that he was within a league of the land. At this distance, the portions of rock and patches of snow, as well as the contour of the different hills, are as distinctly marked as similar objects in many other countries, not having snow about them, would be at a fourth or a fifth part of the distance. Hence we can account, on a reasonable ground, for a curious circumstance related in a Danish voyage, undertaken for the recovery of the last colony in Greenland, by Mogens Heinson. This person, who passed for a renowned seaman in his day, was sent out by Frederick II., king of Denmark. After encountering many difficulties and dangers from storms and ice, he got sight of the east coast of Greenland, and attempted to reach it; but, though the sea was quite free from ice, and the wind favourable and blowing a fresh gale, he, after proceeding several hours without appearing to get any nearer the land, became alarmed, backed about, and returned to Denmark. On his arrival, he attributed this extraordinary circumstance—magnified, no doubt, by his fears—to his vessel having been stopped in its course by "some loadstone rocks hidden in the sea." The true cause, however, of what he took to be a submarine magnetic influence, arose, I doubt not, from the deceptive character of the land, as to distance, which I have mentioned.

Spitzbergen abounds with deep bays and extensive sounds, in many of which are excellent harbours. From Point Look-out to Hackluyt's Headland, the west coast forms almost a series of rocks and foul ground, few parts, excepting the bays, affording anchoring for ships. Some of these rocks are dry only at low water, or only show themselves when the sea is high, and are dangerous to shipping; others are constantly above water, or altogether so below the surface that they can either be seen and avoided, or sailed over in moderate weather without much hazard. On the east side of Point Look-out, a ridge of stony ground stretches five leagues into the sea, towards the south-east, on which the sea occasionally breaks.

Horn Sound affords tolerable anchorage; within Bell Sound are several anchoring places and some rivers, and in Ice Sound, at Green Harbour, is good anchorage near the bank, in ten to eight fathoms' water, or less. In several other places, when not encumbered with ice, there is pretty good refuge for ships. On the north and east sides of Spitzbergen are several harbours, some of them very safe and commodious, but they are not so often free from ice as those westward, and, therefore, have seldom been visited.

Though the whale-fishers in the present age generally see the level of Spitzbergen every voyage, yet not many of them visit the shores. My father has been several times on shore in different parts. My own landing, for the first time in an Arctic country, was on Charles's Island, or Fair Forehead, at the north-west point. The number of birds seen on the precipices and rocks adjoining the sea was immense, and the noise which they made on our approach was quite deafening. The weather was calm and clear when I went on shore, but suddenly, a thick fog and breeze of wind commencing, obliged us to put off with haste, and subjected us to great anxiety before we reached the ship.

In the summer of 1818, I was several times on shore on the main, and landed once in the same season on the north side of King's Bay. Being near the land, on the evening of the 23rd of July, the weather beautifully clear, and all our sails becalmed by the hills, excepting the top-gallant sails, in which we had constantly a gentle breeze, I left the ship in charge of an officer, with orders to stand no nearer than into thirty fathoms' water, and with two boats and fourteen men rowed to the shore. We arrived at the beach about half-past seven, P.M., and landed on a track of low flat ground, extending about six miles north and south, and two or three east and west. This table-land lies so low that it would be overflown by the sea, were it not for a natural embankment of shingle thrown up by the sea.

After advancing about half a furlong, we met with mica slate, in nearly perpendicular strata; and a little further on with an extensive bed of limestone, in small angular fragments. Here and there we saw large ponds of fresh water, derived from melted ice and snow; in some places, small remains of snow; and lastly, near the base of the mountains, a considerable morass, into which we sank nearly to the knees. Some unhealthy-looking mosses appeared on this swamp, but the softest part, as well as most of the ground we had hitherto traversed, was entirely void of vegetation. This swamp had a moorish look, and consisted, apparently, of black alluvial soil, mixed with some vegetable remains, and was curiously marked on the surface with small polygonal ridges, from one to three yards in diameter, so combined as to give the ground an appearance such as that exhibited by a section of honeycomb. An ascent of a few yards from the morass, of somewhat firmer ground, brought us to the foot of the mountain, to the northward of the Mitre Cape. Here some pretty specimens of *Saxifraga oppositifolia* and *Greenlandica*, *Salix herbacea*, *Draba alpina*, *Papaver alpina*, (of Mr. Don,) etc., and some other plants in full flower, were found on little tufts of soil, and scattered about on the ascent. The first hill rose at an inclination of 45°, to the height of about fifteen hundred feet, and was joined on the north side to another of about twice the elevation. We began to climb the acclivity on the most accessible side, at about 10, P.M.; but, from the looseness of the stones, and the steepness of the ascent, we found it a most difficult undertaking. There was scarcely a possibility of advancing by the common movement of walking in this attempt; for the ground gave way at every step, and no progress was made; hence, the only method of succeeding was by the effort of leaping or running, which, under the peculiar circumstances, could not be accomplished without excessive fatigue. In the direction we traversed, we met with angular fragments of limestone and quartz, chiefly of one or two pounds' weight, and a few naked rocks protruding through the loose materials, of which the side of the mountain, to the extent it was visible, was principally composed. These rocks appeared solid at a little distance, but, on examination, were found to be full of fractures in every direction, so that it was with difficulty that a specimen of five or six pounds' weight, in a solid mass, could be obtained. Along the side of the first range of hills, near the summit, was extended a band of ice and snow, which, in the direct ascent, we tried in vain to surmount. By great exertion, however, in tracing the side of the hill for about two hundred yards, where it was so uncommonly steep that at every step showers of stones were precipitated to the bottom, we found a sort of angle of the hill, free from ice, by which the summit was scaled.

Here we rested until I took a few angles and bearings of the most prominent parts of the coast, when, having collected specimens of the minerals, and such few plants as the barren ridge afforded, we proceeded on our excursion. In our way to the principal mountain near us, we passed along a ridge of the secondary mountains, which was so acute that I sat across it with a leg on each side as on horseback. To the very top it consisted of loose sharp limestones, of a yellowish or reddish colour, smaller in size than the stones generally used for repairing high roads, few pieces being above a pound in weight. The fracture appeared rather fresh. After passing along this ridge about three or four furlongs, and crossing a lodgment of ice and snow, we descended by a sort of ravine to the side of the principal mountain, which arose with a uniformly steep ascent, similar to that we had already surmounted, to the very summit. The ascent was now even more difficult than before; we could make no considerable progress, but by the exertion of leaping and running, so that we were obliged to rest after every fifty or sixty paces. No solid rock was met with, and no earth or soil. The stones, however, were larger, appeared more decayed, and were more uniformly covered with black lichens; but several plants of the *Saxifraga, Salix, Draba, Cochlearia,* and *Juncus genera,* which had been met with here and there for the first two thousand feet of elevation, began to disappear as we approached the summit. The invariably broken state of the rocks appeared to have been the effect of frost. On calcareous rocks, some of which are not impervious to moisture, the effect is such as might be expected; but how frost can operate in this way on quartz is not so easily understood.

As we completed the arduous ascent, the sun had just reached the meridian below the Pole, and still shed his reviving rays of unimpaired brilliancy on a small surface of snow, which capped the mountain summit. A thermometer, placed among stones in the shade of the brow of the hill, indicated a temperature as high as 37°. At the top of the first hill, the temperature was 42°; and at the foot, on the plain, 44° to 46°; so that, at the very peak of the mountain, estimated at three thousand feet elevation, the power of the sun at midnight produced a temperature several degrees above the freezing point, and occasioned the discharge of streams of water from the snow-capped summit. In Spitzbergen, the frost relaxes in the months of July and August, and the thawing temperature prevails for considerable intervals on the greatest heights that have been visited.

As the capacity of air for heat increases as its density decreases, and that in such a degree that about every ninety yards of elevation in the lower atmosphere produces a depression of one degree of temperature of Fahrenheit, we find that the elevation of some of the Alps, Pyrenees, and mountains of Nepaul in the temperate zone, is such, that their summits are above the level where a temperature of thawing can at any time prevail; and though, by the application of this principle to the mountains of Spitzbergen, we find that a thawing temperature may be occasionally expected, yet we do not see how the prevalence of a thaw should be so continual as to disperse the winter's coat of snow, where the mean temperature of the hottest month in the year must, on a mountain fifteen hundred feet elevation or upward, probably be below the freezing point. Perhaps the difficulty is to be thus resolved. The weather, in the months of June, July, and August, is much clearer at Spitzbergen than it is near the neighbouring ice, where most of my observations on temperature were made, and as such the temperature of these months on shore must be warmer than at sea, and so much higher indeed as is requisite for occasioning the dissolution of snow even on the tops of the mountains.

The highest temperature I ever observed in Spitzbergen was 48°; but in the summer of 1773, when captain Phipps visited Spitzbergen, a temperature of 58½° once occurred. Supposing this to be the greatest, degree of height which takes place, it will require an elevation of 7,791 feet for reducing that temperature to the freezing point, and hence we may reckon this to be about the altitude of the upper line of congelation, where frost perpetually prevails.

The prospect from the mountain which we ascended was most extensive and grand. A fine sheltered bay was seen on the east of us, an arm of the same on the north-east, and the sea, whose glassy surface was unruffled by the breeze, formed an immense expanse on the west; the icebergs, rearing their proud crests almost to the tops of the mountains between which they were lodged, and defying the power of the solar beams, were scattered in various directions about the sea-coast, and in the adjoining bays. Beds of snow and ice, filling extensive hollows, and giving an enamelled coat to adjoining valleys, one of which, commencing at the foot of the mountain where we stood, extended in a continued line across the north, as far as the eye could reach; mountain rising above mountain, until by distance they dwindled into insignificance; the whole contrasted by a cloudless canopy of deepest azure, and enlightened by the rays of a blazing sun, and the effect aided by a feeling of danger, seated as we were on the pinnacle of a rock, almost surrounded by tremendous precipices; all united to constitute a picture singularly sublime.

A gentle breeze of wind, that prevailed on the summit, much refreshed us, and strengthened us for the descent, which, though we had regarded it with indifference, we found really a very hazardous, and, in some instances, a painful undertaking. On the flat of land next the sea, we met with the horns of reindeer, many skulls and other bones of sea-horses, whales, narwhales, foxes, and seals, and some human skeletons, laid in chest-like coffins, exposed naked on the strand. Two Russian lodges formed of logs of pine, with a third in ruins, were also seen; the former, from a quantity of fresh chips about them, and other appearances, gave evidence of having been recently inhabited. These huts were built upon a ridge of shingle, adjoining the sea. Among the shingle on the beach were numbers of nests, containing the eggs of terns, ducks, and burgomasters, and in some of them were young birds. One of the latter, which we took on board, was very lively, and grew rapidly, but having taken a fancy to a cake of white lead, with which the surgeon was finishing a drawing, he was poisoned. The only insect I saw was a small green fly, which swarmed upon the shingle about the beach. The sea along the coast teemed with a species of *helix*, with the *clio borealis*, and with small shrimps. No animal of the class *Vermes*, and no living quadruped, was observed. Drift-wood was in some abundance, and, owing to the prevalence of a strong west wind, the shore was covered in many places with deep beds of sea-weed.

Of all the objects, however, that we met with in the course of our research, none excited so much interest as the carcase of a dead whale, found stranded on the beach, which, though much swollen, and not a little putrid, fixed our attention, and diverted us from objects of mere curiosity. It proved a prize to us of the value of about £400, but was not secured without much labour. From a harpoon found in its body, it appeared to have been struck by some of the fishers on the Elbe, and having escaped from them, it had probably stranded itself where we found it.

The climate of Spitzbergen is no doubt more disagreeable to human feeling than that of any other country yet discovered. Extending to within ten degrees of the Pole, it is generally intensely cold, and even in the three warmest months, the temperature not averaging more than $34\frac{1}{2}°$, it is then subject to a cold of three, four, or more degrees below the freezing point. It has the advantage, however, of being visited by the sun for an uninterrupted period of four months in each year, thus having a summer's day—if so long an interval between the rising and setting of the sun may be so denominated—consisting of one-third part of the year. But its winter is proportionably desolate; the sun, in the northern parts of the country, remaining perpetually below the horizon from about the 22nd of October to about the 22nd of February. This great winter night, though sufficiently dreary, is by no means so dark as might be expected, God having, by wise and merciful arrangements, distributed, with some approach to equality, the blessings of his providence. The sun, even during its greatest south declination, approaches within $13\frac{1}{2}°$ of the horizon, and affords a faint twilight for about one-fourth part of every twenty-four hours. Added to this twilight, the aurora borealis, which sometimes exhibits a brilliancy approaching a blaze of fire—the stars, which shine with an uncommon degree of brightness—and the moon, which, in north declination, appears for twelve or fourteen days together without setting—altogether have an effect, which, when heightened by the reflection of a constant surface of snow, generally give sufficient light for going abroad; but, with the light afforded by the heavens, when the moon is below the horizon, it is seldom possible to read.

The first human beings who are known to have passed the winter in Spitzbergen, were two parties of seamen, belonging to English whalers, who were left on shore by accident, on two different occasions; the first party, consisting of nine persons, all perished; but the latter, composed of eight individuals, survived the rigours of the winter of 1630-1, and were all rescued. In the year 1633, seven volunteers, belonging to the Dutch fleet, were induced, by certain emoluments, to attempt the same enterprise, and succeeded in passing the winter without sustaining any injury; but, on the same hazardous experiment being tried by seven other persons the following winter, they all fell a sacrifice to the ravages of the scurvy. Some Russians seem to have been the next to attempt this adventurous exploit, who, from being inured to a winter little less severe at home, were enabled to accomplish it with more safety. Four men, who landed on an island on the east side of Spitzbergen, in the year 1743, and were deprived of the means of getting away by an unexpected calamity having overtaken the vessel to which they belonged, remained there some years. Being exposed to uncommon privations, they were led by their necessities to adopt some most ingenious devices for providing themselves with food and raiment in their long and severe banishment. One of their number died; but the others were relieved, after a stay of three years and six months, by a vessel providentially driven on the coast, and restored to their friends, enriched with skins and other produce of the country in which they had been exiled.

In modern times, people of the same nation have been in the habit of submitting to a voluntary transportation, with the object of making some considerable advantage by the opportunities which such a measure affords them of hunting and fishing. These persons were formerly employed in the service of the "White Sea Fishing Company;" but this company being now no longer in existence, the trade is conducted by private adventurers. They now proceed from Megen, Archangel, Onega, Rala, and other places bordering the White Sea, in vessels of sixty to one hundred and sixty tons, some intended for the summer fishing, and others for the winter. The former put to sea in the beginning of June, and sometimes return in September; the latter sail about a month later, and wintering in the most secure coves of Devil Bay, Bell Sound, Horn Sound, Cross Bay, Magdalen Bay, Love Bay, and others, return home in the months of August or September of the following year. The fishermen reside on shore during the winter, in huts of the same kind as those used by the peasants in Russia, which, being taken out with them in pieces, are constructed with but little trouble, in the most convenient situations. They build their stoves with bricks, or with clay, found in the country. Their largest hut, which is erected near the place where their vessels or boats are laid up, is from twenty to twenty-five feet square, and is used as a station and magazine; but the huts used by the men who go in quest of skins, which are erected along shore, are only seven or eight feet square. The smaller huts are usually occupied by two or three men, who take care to provide themselves from the store with the necessary provisions for serving them the whole winter.

I have visited several of these huts, some constructed of logs, others of deals, two inches in thickness. During the stay of the hunters, they employ themselves in killing seals, sea-horses, etc., in the water; and bears, foxes, deer, or whatever else they meet with, on land. They are furnished with provisions for eighteen months by their employers, consisting of rye-flour for bread, oatmeal, barley-meal, peas, salt beef, salt cod, and salt halibut, together with curdled milk, honey, and linseed oil; besides which, they procure for themselves *lion*-deer in winter, and birds in summer. Their drink chiefly consists of a liquor called *nuas*, made from rye-flour and water; malt or spirituous liquors being entirely forbidden, to prevent drunkenness, as these persons, when they were allowed it, drank so immoderately, that their work was often altogether neglected. For general purposes, they use spring water when it is to be had, or, in lieu of it, take water from lakes; but, when neither can be got, they use melted snow. Their fuel, for the most part, is brought with them from Russia, and drift-wood is used for the same purpose. The hunters defend themselves from the rigour of the frost by a covering made of skin, over which they wear a garment called *kushy*, made of the skin of rein-deer, with boots of the same. A warm cap, called a *trucchy*, defends the whole head and neck, and part of the face; and gloves of sheep-skin, the hands. They seldom travel far in winter, but the short excursions they have occasion to make they perform on foot, on snow-skates, and draw their food after them on hand-sledges, but such as have dogs employ them in this service. Their huts, in stormy weather, are often buried in the snow, and in such cases they are obliged to make their way through the chimney to get out. As an anti-scorbutic, they make use of a herb produced in the country, a stock of which they generally provide themselves with on the approach of winter, but sometimes they are under the necessity of digging through the snow to obtain it. They either eat it without any preparation, or drink the liquor prepared from it by infusion in water. For the same purpose, they use a kind of raspberry, and a decoction of fir-tops.

Spitzbergen does not afford many vegetables. It may be remarked, that vegetation goes on uncommonly quick in this country. Most of the plants spring up, flower, and afford seed in the course of a month or six weeks. They are chiefly of a dwarfish size. Some of the flowers are really pretty, but exhibit few colours, excepting yellow, white, and purple. The only plant I met with partaking of the nature of a tree, (a *salix*, allied to *S. herbacea*,) grows but to the height of three or four inches. Although Spitzbergen is probably rich in minerals, yet so partial has been the examination of it that nothing of any value, excepting marble and coal, has yet been met with. The remarks made concerning the appearances and productions of Spitzbergen apply in general to the islands adjacent. The principal of these are Moffen Island, Low Island, Hope Island, and Cherie Island. The last abounds in sea-horses, bears, foxes, and sea-fowl. Lead ore, in veins at the surface, has been found here, and specimens of virgin silver.

Between the latitudes of 70° 49' and 71° 8' 20" north, and between the longitudes 7° 26' and 8° 44', lies the island of Jan Mayen, said to have been first seen by a Dutch navigator of this name in the year 1611. The west side, affording the greatest number of anchorages, having the best convenience for landing, and being better sheltered from the most frequent storms, was selected by the Dutch for their *boiling* stations. I was successful, in my passage homeward, in the year 1817, in effecting a landing. On approaching, the first object which strikes attention is the peak of Beerenberg, which I subsequently saw at a distance (by observation) of ninety-five to a hundred miles. It rears its icy summit to an elevation of 6,780 feet above the level of the sea. After leaving the sea-shore, fragments of lava were seen at every step, and numerous undoubted marks of recent volcanic action. On reaching a summit, estimated at 1,500 feet above the sea, we beheld a beautiful crater, forming a basin of 500 or 600 feet in depth, and 600 or 700 yards in diameter. The bottom of the crater was filled with alluvial matter to such a height that it presented a horizontal flat of an elliptical form, measuring 400 feet by 240. In the spring of the following year, some volcano was, I believe, in action in this neighbourhood, as I observed considerable jets of smoke discharged from the earth at intervals of every three or four minutes.

CHAPTER III.

AN ACCOUNT OF THE GREENLAND OR POLAR ICE.

Of the inanimate productions of the Polar Seas, none perhaps excite so much interest and astonishment in a stranger as the ice in its great abundance and variety. The stupendous masses known by the name of icelands or icebergs, common to Davis's Strait, and sometimes met with in the Spitzbergen Sea, from their height, various forms, and the depth of water in which they ground, are calculated to strike the beholder with wonder; yet the prodigious sheets of ice, called ice-fields, more peculiar to the Spitzbergen Sea, are not less astonishing. Their deficiency in elevation is sufficiently compensated by their amazing extent of surface. Some of them have been observed extending many leagues in length, and covering an area of several hundreds of square miles, each consisting of a single sheet of ice, having its surface raised in general four or six feet above the level of the water, and its base depressed to the depth of ten to twenty feet beneath.

The ice in general is designated by a variety of appellations, distinguishing it according to the size or shape of the pieces, their number or form of aggregation, thickness, transparency, situation, etc. As the different denominations of ice will be frequently referred to in the course of this work, it may be useful to give definitions of the terms in use among the whale-fishers for distinguishing them.

1. An *iceberg*, or ice-mountain, is a large insulated peak of floating ice, or a glacier, occupying a ravine or valley, generally opening towards the sea in an arctic country.

2. A *field* is a sheet of ice, so extensive that its limits cannot be discerned from the ship's mast-head.

3. A *floe* is similar to a field, but smaller, inasmuch as its extent *can* be seen. This term, however, is seldom applied to pieces of ice of less diameter than half-a-mile or a mile.

4. *Drift-ice* consists of pieces less than floes, of various shapes and magnitudes.

5. *Brash-ice* is still smaller than drift-ice, and may be considered as the wreck of other kinds of ice.

6. *Bay-ice* is that which is newly-formed on the sea, and consists of two kinds, common bay-ice and *pancake*-ice; the former occurring in smooth extensive sheets, and the latter in small circular pieces, with raised edges.

7. *Sludge* consists of a stratum of detached ice crystals, or of snow, or of the smaller fragments of brash-ice, floating on the surface of the sea.

8. A *hummock* is a protuberance raised upon any plane of ice above the common level. It is frequently produced by pressure, where one piece is squeezed upon another, often set upon its edge, and in that position cemented by the frost. Hummocks are likewise formed by pieces of ice mutually crushing each other, the wreck being heaped upon one or both of them. To hummocks, principally, the ice is indebted for its variety of fanciful shapes, and its picturesque appearance. They occur in great numbers in heavy packs, on the edges, and occasionally in the middle of fields and floes, where they often attain the height of thirty feet or upwards.

9. A *calf* is a portion of ice which has been depressed by the same means as a hummock is elevated. It is kept down by some larger mass, from beneath which it shows itself on one side.

10. A *tongue* is a point of ice projecting nearly horizontally from a part that is under water. Ships have sometimes run aground upon tongues of ice.

11. A *pack* is a body of drift-ice, of such magnitude that its extent is not discernible. A pack is *open* when the pieces of ice, though very near each other, do not generally touch, or *close* when the pieces are in complete contact.

12. A *patch* is a collection of drift or bay-ice, of a circular or polygonal form. In point of magnitude, a pack corresponds with a field, and a patch with a floe.

13. A *stream* is an oblong collection of drift or bay-ice, the pieces of which are continuous. It is called a *sea-stream* when it is exposed on one side to the ocean, and affords shelter from the sea to whatever is within it.

14. *Open-ice*, or *sailing-ice*, is where the pieces are so separate as to admit of a ship sailing conveniently among them.

15. *Heavy* and *light* are terms attached to ice, distinguishable of its thickness.

16. *Land-ice* consists of drift-ice attached to the shore; or drift-ice which, by being covered with mud or gravel, appears to have recently been in contact with the shore; or the flat ice resting on the land, not having the appearance or elevation of icebergs.

17. A *bight* is a bay in the outline of the ice.

18. A *lane* or *vein* is a narrow channel of water in packs or other large collections of ice.

When the sea freezes, the greatest part of the salt it contains is deposited, and the frozen mass, however spongy, probably contains no salt but what is natural to the sea-water filling its pores. Hence the generality of ice, when dissolved, affords fresh water. As, however, the ice frozen altogether from sea-water does not appear so solid and transparent as that procured from snow or rain water, the whale-fishers distinguish it into two kinds, accordingly as it affords water that is potable, or the contrary, as it appears to have been the product of fresh or salt water.

What is considered as salt-water-ice appears blackish in the water, but in the air is of a white or grey colour, porous, and in a great measure opaque, (except when in very thin pieces,) yet transmits the rays of light with a blue or blueish green shade. When dissolved, it produces water sometimes perfectly fresh, and at others saltish. This depends, in a great measure, on the situation from whence it is taken; such parts as are raised above the surface of the sea, in the form of hummocks, or which, though below the surface, have been long frozen, appear to gain solidity, and are commonly *fresh*; whilst those pieces taken out of the sea, that have been recently frozen, are somewhat salt.

Fresh-water-ice of the sailors is distinguished by its black appearance when floating in small pieces in the sea, and by its transparency when removed into the air. Fresh-water-ice is fragile, but hard; the edges of a fractured part are frequently so keen as to inflict a wound like glass. The most transparent pieces are capable of concentrating the rays of the sun, so as to produce a considerable intensity of heat. With a lump of ice, of by no means regular convexity, I have frequently burned wood, fired gunpowder, incited lead, and lit the sailors' pipes, to their great astonishment, all of whom, who could procure the needful articles, eagerly flocked around me, for the satisfaction of smoking a pipe ignited by such extraordinary means. Their astonishment was increased by observing that the ice remained firm and pellucid, while the solar rays emerging from it were so hot, that the hand could not be kept longer in the focus than for the space of a few seconds. In the formation of these lenses, I roughed them out with a small axe, and then scraped them with a knife, polishing them merely by the warmth of the hand, supporting them during the operation in a woollen glove. I once procured a piece of the purest ice, so large that a lens of sixteen inches diameter was obtained out of it; unhappily, however, the sun became obscured before it was completed, and never made its appearance again for a fortnight, during which time, the air being mild, the lens was spoiled.

All young ice, such as bay-ice and light-ice, which form a considerable part of drift and pack-ice in general, is considered by Greenland sailors salt-water-ice; while fields, floes, bergs, and heavy-ice, chiefly consist of fresh-water-ice. Brash-ice likewise affords fine specimens of the latter, which, when taken out of the sea, are always found crowded on the surface with sharp points and conchoidal excavations.

Ice, when rapidly dissolved, continues solid as long as any remains, but, when exposed to the air, at a temperature of only two or three degrees above the freezing point, its solution is effected in a very peculiar manner. Thus, a large lump of fresh-water-ice, when acted on by such a process, if placed in the plane of its formation, resolves itself into considerable columns of a prismatic appearance. These columns are situated in a perpendicular position, almost entirely detached, so that when a blow is struck with an axe, the whole mass frequently falls to pieces. In the land icebergs, these columns are often of amazing magnitude, so as, when separated, to form floating icebergs.

All the ice floating in the sea is generally rough and uneven on the surface, and during the greater part of the year covered with snow. Even newly-formed ice, which is free from snow, is so rough and soft that it cannot be skated upon. Under water the colour of the ice varies with the colour of the sea; in blue water it is blue, in green water it is green, and of deeper shades in proportion to its depth. In the thickest olive-green coloured water, its colour, far beneath the surface, appears brownish.

A description of the process of freezing from its commencement may now be attempted. The first appearance of ice, when in a state of detached crystals, is called by the sailors *sludge*, and resembles snow when cast into water that is too cold to dissolve it. This smooths the ruffled surface of the sea, and produces an effect like oil in preventing breakers. These crystals soon unite, and would form a continuous sheet, but, by the motion of the waves, they are broken in very small pieces, scarcely three inches in diameter. As they strengthen, many of them coalesce, and form a larger mass. The undulations of the sea still continuing, these enlarged pieces strike each other on every side, whereby they become rounded, and their edges turn up, whence they obtain the name of *cakes*, or *pan-cakes*. Several of these again unite, and thereby continue to increase, forming larger flakes, until they become perhaps a foot in thickness, and many yards in circumference. Every larger flake retains on its surface the impression of the smaller flakes of which it is composed, so that when, by the discontinuance of the swell, the whole is permitted to freeze into an extensive sheet, it sometimes assumes the appearance of a pavement. But when the sea is perfectly smooth, the freezing process goes on more regularly, and probably more rapidly. During twenty-four hours' keen frost, the ice will become an inch or two in thickness, and in less than forty-eight hours' time capable of sustaining the weight of a man. Both this kind, and cake-ice, are termed bay-ice. In every opening of the main body of ice at a distance from the sea, the water is always as smooth as that of a harbour; and in low temperatures, all that is necessary for the formation of ice is still water. There is no doubt that a large quantity of ice is annually generated in the bays and amidst the islands of Spitzbergen; which bays, towards the end of summer, are commonly emptied of their contents, from the thawing of the snow on the mountains causing a current outwards. But this will not account for the immense fields which are so abundant in

Greenland. These evidently come from the northward, and have their origin between Spitzbergen and the Pole.

Ice-fields constitute one of the wonders of the deep. They are often met with of the diameter of twenty or thirty miles, and when in the state of such close combination that no interstice could be seen, they sometimes extend to a length of fifty or a hundred miles. The ice of which they are composed is generally pure and fresh, and in heavy fields it is probably of the average thickness of ten to fifteen feet, and then appears to be flat, low, thin ice; but when high hummocks occur, the thickness is often forty feet and fifty feet. The surface before the month of July is always covered with a bed of snow, from perhaps a foot to a fathom in depth. This snow dissolves in the end of summer, and forms extensive pools and lakes of fresh water. Some of the largest fields are very level and smooth, though generally their surfaces are varied with hummocks. In some, these hummocks form ridges or chains, in others, they consist of insulated heaps. I once saw a field which was so free from either fissure or hummock, that I imagined, had it been free from snow, a coach might have been driven many leagues over it in a direct line, without obstruction or danger. Hummocks somewhat relieve the uniformity of intense light reflected from the surface of fields, by exhibiting shades of delicate blue in all the hollows, where the light is partly intercepted by passing through a portion of ice.

When the surface of snow on fields is frozen, or when the snow is generally dissolved, there is no difficulty in travelling over them, even without snow-skates or sledges. But when the snow is soft and deep, travelling on foot to any distance is a work of labour. The tribe of Esquimaux, discovered by captain Ross, made use of sledges, drawn by dogs, for conveying them across the rough land-ice, lying between the ships and the shore. A journey they performed with such celerity, that captain Ross conjectured they could travel fifty or sixty miles a day. If such a distance were practicable on drift-ice, occurring near shore, it would be much more easy on the smoother ice of fields.

This term, *field*, was given to the largest sheets of ice by a Dutch whale-fisher. It was not until a period of many years after the Spitzbergen fishery was established, that any navigator attempted to penetrate the ice, or that any of the most extensive sheets of ice were seen. One of the ships resorting to Smeerenberg for fishery, put to sea on one occasion when no whales were seen, persevered westward to a considerable length, and accidentally fell in with some immense flakes of ice, which, on his return to his companions, he described as truly wonderful, and as resembling fields in the extent of their surface. Hence the application of the term field to this kind of ice. The discoverer of it was distinguished by the title of "field-finder."

Fields commonly make their appearance in the months of May or June, though sometimes earlier; they are frequently the resort of young whales. Strong north and westerly winds expose them to the whalers by driving off the loose ice. The invariable tendency of fields is to drift to the southwestward, even in calms, which is the means of many being yearly destroyed. They have frequently been observed to advance a hundred miles in this direction within the space of one month, notwithstanding the occurrence of winds from every quarter. On emerging from amidst the smaller ice, which before sheltered them, they are soon broken up by the swell, are partly dissolved, and partly converted into drift-ice. The places of such are supplied by others from the north. The power of the swell in breaking the heaviest fields is not a little remarkable. A grown swell, that is so inconsiderable as not to be observed in open water, frequently breaks up the largest fields, and converts them wholly into floes and drift-ice in the space of a few hours; while fields composed of bay-ice, or light-ice, being more flexible, endure the same swell without any destructive effort.

The occasional rapid motion of fields, with the strange effects produced by such immense bodies on any opposing substance, is one of the most striking objects the Polar seas present, and is certainly the most terrific. They not unfrequently acquire a rotatory movement, whereby their circumference attains a velocity of several miles per hour. A field thus in motion, coming in contact with another at rest, or more especially with another having a contrary direction of movement, produces a dreadful shock. A body of more than ten thousand millions of tons in weight, meeting with resistance when in motion, produces consequences which it is scarcely possible to conceive. The weaker field is crushed with an awful noise; sometimes the destruction is mutual; pieces of huge dimensions and weight are not unfrequently piled upon the top, to the height of twenty or thirty feet, while a proportionate quantity is depressed beneath. The view of these stupendous effects in *safety* exhibits a picture sublimely grand, but where there is danger of being overwhelmed, terror and dismay must be the predominant feelings. The whale-fishers at all times require unremitting vigilance to secure their safety, but scarcely in any situation so much as when navigating amidst these fields; in foggy weather, they are particularly dangerous, as their motions cannot then be distinctly observed. It may easily be imagined, that the strongest ship is but an insignificant impediment between two fields in motion. Numbers of vessels, since the establishment of the fishery, have been thus destroyed; some have been thrown upon the ice, some have had their hulls completely torn open, or divided in two, and others have been overrun by the ice, and buried beneath its heaped fragments. The Dutch have lost as many as twenty-three sail of ships among the ice in one year. In the season of 1684, fourteen of their ships were wrecked, and eleven more remained beset during the winter.

In the month of May, of the year 1814, I witnessed a tremendous scene. While navigating amidst the most ponderous ice which the Greenland Sea presents, in the prospect of making our escape from a state of *besetment*, our progress was unexpectedly arrested by an isthmus of ice, about a mile in breadth, formed by the coalition of the point of an immense field on the north, with that of an aggregation of floes on the south. To the north field we moored the ship, in the hope of the ice separating in this place. I then quitted the ship, and travelled over the ice to the point of collision, to observe the state of the bar, which now prevented our release. I immediately discovered that the two points had but recently met, that already a prodigious mass of rubbish had been squeezed upon the top, and that the motion had not abated. The fields continued to overlay each other with a majestic motion, producing a noise resembling that of complicated machinery, or distant thunder. The pressure was so immense, that numerous fissures were occasioned, and the ice repeatedly rent beneath my feet. In one of the fissures, I found the snow on the level three and a half feet deep, and the ice upwards of twelve. In one place, hummocks had been thrown up to the height of twenty feet from the surface of the field, and at least twenty-five feet from the level of the water; they extended fifty or sixty yards in length, and fifteen in breadth, forming a mass of about two thousand tons in weight. The majestic, unvaried movement of the ice, the singular noise by which it was accompanied, the tremendous power exerted, and the wonderful effects produced—were calculated to excite in the mind of the most careless spectator admiration of Him with whom "the nations are as a drop of a bucket, and are counted as the small dust of the balance: behold, he taketh up the isles as a very little thing."

The term *icebergs* has commonly been applied to the glaciers occurring in Spitzbergen, Greenland, and other arctic countries. It is also as commonly extended to the large peaks, mountains, or islets of ice that are found floating in the sea. It is the latter kind of icebergs we purpose to describe.

Icebergs occur in many places in the arctic and antarctic regions; some of them of astonishing magnitude. In the Spitzbergen Sea, indeed, they are neither numerous nor bulky, compared with those of other regions; the largest I ever met with in this quarter not exceeding a thousand yards in circumference, and two hundred feet in thickness. But in Hudson's Strait, Davis's Strait, and Baffin's Bay, they occur of a prodigious size. Ellis describes them as sometimes occurring of the thickness of five hundred or six hundred yards. Frobisher saw one iceberg which was judged to be "near fourscore fathoms above water." One berg is described by captain Ross (the dimensions of which were given in by lieutenant Parry[1]) as having nine unequal sides, as being aground in sixty-one fathoms, and as measuring 4,169 yards (paces) long, 3,689 yards broad, and fifty-one feet high. The weight of this iceberg, taken at somewhat smaller dimensions, was estimated, by an officer of the Alexander, at 1,292,397,673 tons. This amount, however, is greater than the truth, the cubical inch of ice being taken at 240 grains, whereas it does not exceed 231·5 grains.

The most abundant source of icebergs known in the arctic regions is Baffin's Bay. From this remarkable sea they constantly make their way towards the south, down Davis's Strait, and are scattered abroad in the Atlantic to an amazing extent. The banks of Newfoundland are occasionally crowded with these wonderful productions of the frigid zone; beyond which they are sometimes conveyed, by the operation of the southerly under-current, as low as latitude 40° north, and even lower, a distance of at least two thousand miles from the place of their origin.

Icebergs commonly float on a base which is larger in extent than the upper surface. Hence the proportion of ice appearing above water is seldom less in elevation than one-seventh of the whole thickness; and when the summit is conical, the elevation above water is frequently one-fourth of the whole depth of the berg. Perhaps the most general form of icebergs is with one high perpendicular side, the opposite side very low, and the intermediate surface forming a gradual slope. When of such a form, captain Ross found that the higher end was generally to windward. Some icebergs have regular flat surfaces, but most usually they have different acute summits, and occasionally exhibit the most fantastic shapes. Some have been seen that were completely perforated, or containing prodigious caverns, or having many clefts or cracks in the most elevated parts, so as to give the appearance of several distinct spires. On some icebergs, where there are hollows, a great quantity of snow accumulates; others are smooth and naked. The naked sides are often filled with conchoidal excavations, of various magnitudes; sometimes with hollows the size of the finger, and as regular as if formed by art. On some bergs, pools of water occur stagnant; on others, large streams are seen oozing through crevices into the sea. In a high sea, the waves break against them as against a rock; and, in calm weather, where there is a swell, the noise made by their rising and falling is tremendous. When icebergs are aground, or when there is a superficial current running to leeward, the motion of other ice past them is so great that they appear to be moving to windward. Fields of ice, of considerable thickness, meeting a berg under such circumstances, are sometimes completely ripped up and divided through the middle. Icebergs, when acted on by the sun, or by a temperate atmosphere, become hollow and fragile. Large pieces are then liable to be broken off, and fall into the sea with a terrible crash, which, in some places, produces an echo in the neighbouring mountains. When this circumstance, called *calving*, takes place, the iceberg loses its equilibrium, sometimes turns on one side, and is occasionally inverted. The sea is thereby put into commotion, fields of ice in the vicinity are broken up, the waves extend, and the noise is heard to the distance of several miles; and sometimes the rolling motion of the berg not ceasing, other pieces get loosened and detached, till the whole mass falls asunder like a wreck.

Icebergs differ a little in colour according to their solidity and distance, or state of the atmosphere. A very general appearance is that of cliffs of chalk, or of white or grey marble. The sun's rays reflected from them sometimes give a glistening appearance to their surfaces. Different shades of colour occur in the precipitous parts, accordingly as the ice is more or less solid, and accordingly as it contains strata of earth, gravel, or sand, or is free from any impurity. In the fresh fracture, greenish grey, approaching to emerald green, is the prevailing colour. In the night, icebergs are readily distinguished, even at a distance, by their natural effulgence; and in foggy weather, by a peculiar blackness in the atmosphere, by which the danger to the navigator is diminished. As, however, they occur far from land, and often in unexpected situations, navigators require to be always on the watch for them. Though often dangerous neighbours, they have occasionally proved useful auxiliaries to the whale-fishers. Their situation in a smooth sea is very little affected by the wind; under the strongest gale they are not perceptibly moved, but, on the contrary, have the appearance of advancing to windward, because every other description of ice moves rapidly past them. From the iceberg's firmness, it often affords a stable mooring to the ship in strong adverse winds, and the fisher likewise avails himself of it when his object is to gain a windward situation more open. He moors under the lee of the iceberg, loose ice soon forces past, the ship remains nearly stationary, and the wished-for effect seldom fails to result. Vessels have, however, often been staved, and sometimes wrecked, by the fall of their icy mooring; while smaller objects, such as boats, have been repeatedly overwhelmed, even at a considerable distance, by the vast waves occasioned by such events.

All ice becomes exceedingly fragile towards the close of the whale-fishing season, when the temperate air thaws its surface, and changes its solid structure into a brittle mass of imperfectly attached columns. Bergs in this state being struck by an axe, for the purpose of placing a mooring anchor, have been known to rend asunder, and precipitate the careless seaman into the yawning chasm; whilst, occasionally, the masses are hurled apart, and fall in contrary directions with a prodigious crash, burying boats and men in one common ruin. The awful effect produced by a solid mass, many thousands, or even millions, of tons in weight, changing its situation with the velocity of a falling body, whereby its aspiring summit is in a moment buried in the ocean, can be more easily imagined than described. Though a blow with an edge-tool on brittle ice does not sever the mass, still it is often succeeded by a crackling noise, proving the mass to be ready to burst from the force of internal expansion, or from the destruction of its texture by a warm temperature. It is common, when ships moor to icebergs, to lie as remote from them as their ropes will allow, and yet accidents sometimes happen, though the ship ride at the distance of a hundred yards from the ice. In the year 1812, while the Thomas, of Hull, captain Taylor, lay moored to an iceberg in Davis's Strait, a *calf* was detached from beneath, and rose with such tremendous force, that the keel of the ship was lifted on a level with water at the bow, and the stern was nearly immersed beneath the surface. Fortunately, the blow was received on the keel, and the ship was not materially damaged.

From the deep pools of water found in the summer season on the depressed surface of some bergs, or from streams running down their sides, the ships navigating where they abound are presented with opportunities for watering with the greatest ease and dispatch. For this purpose, casks are landed upon the lower bergs, filled, and rolled into the sea; but, from the higher, the water is conveyed by means of a long tube of canvas, or leather, called a *hose*, into casks placed in the boats, at the side of the ice, or even upon the deck of the ship.

The greater part of the icebergs that occur in Davis's Strait, and on the eastern coast of North America, notwithstanding their profusion and immense magnitude, seem to be merely fragments of the land icebergs, or glaciers, which exist in great numbers on the coast forming the boundaries of Baffin's Bay. These glaciers fill immense valleys, and extend, in some places, several miles into the sea; in others, they terminate with a precipitous edge at the general line formed by the coast. In the summer season, when they are particularly fragile, the force of cohesion is often overcome by the weight of the prodigious masses that overhang the sea; and, in winter, the same effect may be produced by the powerful expansion of the water filling any excavation, or deep-seated cavity, when its dimensions are enlarged by freezing, thereby exerting a tremendous force, and bursting the berg asunder. Pieces thus, or otherwise, detached, are hurled into the sea with a dreadful crash. When they fall into sufficiently deep water, they are liable to be drifted off the land, and down Davis's Strait, according to the set of the current; but, if they fall into a shallow sea, they must remain until sufficiently wasted to float away.

Spitzbergen is possessed of every character which is supposed to be necessary for the formation of the largest icebergs; high mountains, deep extensive valleys, intense frost, occasional thaws, and great falls of sleet and snow; yet here a berg is rarely met with, and the largest that occur are not to be compared with the productions of Baffin's Bay. The reason of the difference between Spitzbergen and Old Greenland as to the production of icebergs is, perhaps, this—that, while the sea is generally deep, and the coast almost continually sheltered by drift-ice at the foot of the glaciers, in Baffin's

Bay; in Spitzbergen, on the contrary, they usually terminate at the water's edge, or where the sea is shallow, so that no very large mass, if dislodged, can float away, and they are, at the same time, so much exposed to heavy swells, as to occasion dismemberments too frequently to admit of their attaining considerable magnitude.

That extensive body of ice which, with occasional tracts of land, occupies the northern extremity of the earth, and prevents all access to the regions immediately surrounding the Pole, fills, it appears, on an average, a circle of above two thousand geographical miles diameter, and presents an outline which, though subject to partial variations, is found at the same season of each succeeding year to be generally similar, and often strikingly uniform. The most remarkable alteration in the configuration of the Polar ice on record, is that said to have taken place between Iceland and Greenland, in the beginning of the fifteenth century, whereby the intercourse between the Icelanders and the colonies in Greenland was interrupted; and, although many attempts have been made on the part of Denmark for the recovery of these colonies, and for ascertaining the fate of the colonists, they have not yet succeeded. In various countries, changes of climate, to a certain extent, have occurred within the limits of historical record; these changes have been commonly for the better, and have been considered as the effects of human industry, in draining marshes and lakes, felling woods, and cultivating the earth; but here is an occurrence which, if it be indeed true, is the reverse of common experience, and concerning the causes of which it is not easy to offer any conjecture.

With each recurring spring, the north Polar ice presents the following general outline. Filling the Bays of Hudson and Baffin, as well as the Straits of Hudson, and part of that of Davis, it exhibits an irregular, waving, but generally continuous line, from Newfoundland or Labrador to Nova Zembla. From Newfoundland it extends in a northerly direction along the Labrador shore, generally preventing all access to the land, as high as the mouth of Hudson's Strait; then, turning to the north-eastward, forms a bay near the coast of Greenland, in latitude perhaps 66° or 67°, by suddenly passing away to the southward to the extremity of Greenland. The quantity of ice on the east side of Davis's Strait being often small, the continuity of its border is liable to be broken, so as to admit of ships reaching the land; and sometimes the bay of the ice, usually occurring in the spring, in latitude 66° or 67°, does not exist, but the sea is open up the strait to a considerable distance beyond it. After doubling the southern promontory, or Cape Farewell, it advances in a north-eastern direction along the east coast, sometimes enveloping Iceland as it proceeds, until it reaches the Island of Jan Mayen. Passing this island on the north-west, but frequently inclosing it, the edge of the ice then trends a little more to the eastward, and usually intersects the meridian of London between the 71st and 73rd degree of latitude. Having reached the longitude of 5° or 6° east, in some instances as far as 8° or 10°, in the 73rd or 74th degree or north latitude, it joins a remarkable promontory, and suddenly stretches to the north, sometimes proceeding on a meridian to the latitude of 80°, at others forming a deep sinuosity, extending two or three degrees to the northward, and then south-easterly to Cherie Island, which, having passed, it assumes a more direct course a little to the southward of east, until it forms a junction with the Siberian or Nova Zemblan coast.

During the winter and spring months, the Polar ice seems closely to embrace the whole of the northern shores of Russia, to the eastward of Nova Zembla, and filling, in a great measure, Behring's Strait and the sea to the northward of it, continues in contact with the Polar face of the American continent, following the line of the coast to the eastward, until it effects a junction with the ice in the Spitzbergen Sea, or in the great north-western bays of Hudson and Baffin, or is terminated by land yet undiscovered.

That remarkable promontory midway between Jan Mayen and Cherie Islands, formed by the sudden stretch of the ice to the north, constitutes the line of separation between the east, or *whaling*, and west, or *sealing*, ice of the fishers; and the deep bay lying to the east of this promontory, which may be called the *Whale-fisher's Bight*, invariably forms the only pervious track for proceeding to fishing latitudes northward. When the ice at the extremity of this bay occurs so strong and compact as to prevent the approach to the shores of Spitzbergen, and the advance northward beyond the latitude of 75° or 76°, it is said to be a *close season*, and, on the contrary, it is called an *open season* when an uninterrupted navigation extends along the western coast of Spitzbergen to Hackluyt's Headland.

The place where whales occur in the greatest abundance is generally found to be in 78° or 79° of north latitude, though, from the 72nd to the 81st degree they have been met with. They prefer those situations which afford them the most secure retreats, and the course of their flight when scared or wounded is generally towards the nearest or most compact ice. The place of their retreat, however, is regulated by various circumstances; it may sometimes depend on the quality or quantity of food occurring, the disposition of the ice, or exemption from enemies. Sometimes they seem collected within a small and single circuit; at others, they are scattered in various hordes and numerous single individuals over an amazing extent of surface. In *close seasons*, though the ice joins the south of Spitzbergen, and thereby forms a *barrier* against the fishing-stations, yet this barrier is often of a limited extent, and terminates on the coasts of Spitzbergen in an open space, either forming or leading to the retreat of the whales. Such space is sometimes frozen over till the middle or end of the month of May, but not unfrequently free from ice. The barrier here opposed to the fisher usually consists of a body of ice, from twenty to thirty or forty leagues across in the shortest diameter. It is of importance to pass this barrier of ice as early as possible in the season. The fisher here avails himself of every power within his command. The sails are expanded in favourable winds, and withdrawn in contrary breezes. The ship is urged forward amongst drift-ice by the force of the wind, assisted with ropes and saws. Whenever a vein of water appears in the required direction, it is, if possible, attained. It always affords a temporary relief, and sometimes a permanent release, by extending itself through intricate mazes, amidst ice of various descriptions, until at length it opens into the desired place, void of obstruction, constituting the usual retreat of the whales.

The barrier which we have described, when it occurs, is regularly encountered on the first arrival of the Greenland ships in the month of April, but is generally removed by natural means as the season advances. It is usually found separate from the land, and divided asunder by the close of the month of June; and hence it is that, however difficult and laborious may have been the ingress into the fishing country, the egress is commonly effected without much inconvenience. In the month of May, the severity of the frost relaxes, and the temperature generally approaches a few degrees of the freezing point. The salt in the sea then exerts its liquefying influence, and destroys the tenacity of the bay-ice, makes inroads in its parts by enlarging its pores into holes, diminishes its thickness, and, in the language of the whale-fisher, completely rots it. Packed drift-ice is then liberated, and obeys the slightest impulses of the winds or currents. The heavier having more stability than the lighter, an apparent difference of movement obtains among the pieces, and holes and lanes of water are formed to allow the entrance and progress of the ships. Bay-ice, though sometimes serviceable to the whalers in preserving them from the brunt of the heavy ice, is often the means of besetment, and hence the primary cause of every calamity. Heavy ice, many feet in thickness, and in detached pieces of from fifty to a hundred tons' weight each, though crowded together in the form of a pack, may be penetrated in a favourable gale with tolerable dispatch, whilst a sheet of bay-ice, of a few inches only in thickness, with the same advantage of wind, will often arrest the progress of the ship, and render her in a few minutes immovable. If this ice be too strong to be broken by the weight of the boat, recourse must be had to sawing, an operation slow and laborious in the extreme.

When the warmth of the season has rotted the bay-ice, the passage to the northward can generally be accomplished with a very great saving of labour. Therefore it was the older fishers seldom or never used to attempt it before the 10th of May, and foreign fishers in the present day are in general late.

Sometimes late arrivals are otherwise beneficial, since it frequently happens, in *close seasons*, that ships entering the ice about the middle of May obtain an advantage over those preceding them, by gaining a situation more eligible, on account of its nearness to the land. Their predecessors, meanwhile, are drifted off to the westward with the ice, and cannot recover their easting. Hence, it appears, it would be economical and beneficial to sail so late as not to reach the *country* before the middle of May, or to persevere on the sealing stations until that time. There are, however, some weighty objections to this method. Open seasons occasionally occur, and great progress may be made, especially by superior fishers, before that time. A week or a fortnight's solitary fishing, under favourable circumstances, has frequently gained half a cargo. The change which takes place in the ice, amidst which the whale-fisher pursues his object, is, towards the close of the *season*, indeed astonishing. For, not only does it separate into its original individual portions, not only does it retreat in a body from the western coast of Spitzbergen, but, in general, that barrier of ice which incloses the fishing-site in the spring, which costs the fisher immense labour and anxiety to penetrate, by retarding his advance towards the north, and his progress in the fishery, for the space of several weeks, spontaneously divides in the midst about the month of June, and, on the return of the ships, is not at all to be seen. Then is the sea rendered freely navigable from the very haunts of the whales to the expanse of the Atlantic Ocean.

Our remarks may now be directed, for a few pages, to the properties, peculiar movements, and drifting of the ice.

1. The ice always has a tendency to separate during calms.

2. Openings in packs and among fields, or floes, frequently break out, or disappear, without any apparent cause.

3. Fields often open, close, and revolve, in the most extraordinary manner, in calms as well as in storms.

4. The amazing changes which take place amongst the most compact ice are often unaccountable.

5. When speaking of the currents of the Spitzbergen Sea, it has been remarked that the Polar ice, in this situation, has a constant tendency to drift to the south-westward. Near Spitzbergen, indeed, this tendency is not usually observed, because the influence of the tide, eddies, peculiar pressures, etc., sometimes produce a contrary effect; but, at a distance from land, its universal prevalence is easily illustrated.

In the beginning of May, 1814, we entered with the ship Esk, of Whitby, a spacious opening of the ice, in latitude 78° 10', longitude 4° east, to a distance of ten or twelve leagues from the exterior, wherein we were tempted to stay, from the appearance of a great number of whales. On the 9th of May, the ship became fixed in the ice, and, until the 16th, we lay immovable. A break of the bay-ice then appeared about half-a-mile from us, to attain which we laboured with energy, and, in eight hours, accomplished a passage for the ship. On the 20th, in attempting to advance, we endured a heavy pressure of the bay-ice, which shook the ship in an alarming manner. After a fatiguing effort in passing through the midst of an aggregation of floes against the wind, we reached a channel, which led us several miles to the south-eastward; and, on the 23rd, we lay at rest with four other ships. The day following, having sawn a place for the ship in a thin floe, we forced forward between two large masses, where bay-ice, unconsolidated, had been compressed till it had become ten or twelve feet thick. We were assisted by a hundred men from the accompanying ships, which followed close in our rear. After applying all our mechanical powers during eight or nine hours, we passed the strait of about a furlong in length, and immediately the ice collapsed, and riveted the ships of our companions to the spot. We advanced on various winding courses to the distance of several miles, and then discovered a continuation of the navigation between two immense sheets of ice, but the channel was so narrow and intricate, that, for the distance of near a mile, it did not appear more than from ten to twenty yards in width. The prospect was, indeed, appalling; but, perceiving indications of the enlargement of the passage rather than the contrary, we advanced under a press of sail, driving aside some disengaged lumps of ice that opposed us, and shortly accomplished our wishes in safety. Here an enlivening prospect presented itself; to the extreme limits of the horizon no interruption was visible. We made a predetermined signal to the ships we had left, indicative of our hope of speedy release. In two hours, however, we were disappointed by meeting the fields in the act of collapsing, and completely barring our progress. As the distance across was scarcely a mile, and the sea, to appearance, clear beyond it, the interruption was most tantalizing. We waited at the point of union, and, on the morning of the 26th of May, our anxiety was happily relieved by the wished-for division of the ice. The ship, propelled by a brisk wind, darted through the strait, and entered a sea, which we considered the termination of our difficulties. After steering three hours to the south-eastward, we were concerned to discover our conclusions had been premature. An immense pack opened on our view, stretching directly across our path. There was no alternative but forcing through it; we therefore pushed forward into the least connected part. By availing ourselves of every advantage of sailing, where sailing was practicable, and *boring* or drifting where the pieces of ice lay close together, we at length reached the leeward part of a narrow channel, in which we had to ply a considerable distance against the wind. When performing this, the wind, which had hitherto blown a brisk breeze from the north, increased to a strong gale. The ship was placed in such a critical situation that we could not, for above an hour, accomplish any reduction of the sails; and while I was personally engaged performing the duty of a pilot on the topmast-head, the bending of the mast was so uncommon that I was seriously alarmed for its stability. At length, we were enabled to reef our sails, and for some time proceeded with less danger. Our direction was now east, then north for several hours, then easterly, ten or fifteen miles; when, after eighteen hours of the most difficult and occasionally hazardous sailing, in which the ship received some hard blows from the ice, after pursuing a tedious course nearly ninety miles, and accomplishing a distance on a direct north-east course of about forty miles, we found ourselves at the very margin of the sea, separated only by a narrow sea-stream. The sea was so great without, and the wind so violent, that we durst not hazard an attempt to force through this remaining obstacle. After waiting about thirty hours, on the morning of the 28th of May, the weather cleared, and the wind abated. The sea-stream was now augmented to upwards of a mile broad. One place alone was visible where the breadth was less considerable, and through it we accomplished our final escape into the open sea.

I have thus been minute in the relation of our extrication from an alarming, though not very uncommon state of besetment, in order to give a faint idea of the difficulties and dangers which those engaged in the whale-fishery have occasionally to encounter, as well as to illustrate the manner in which ships are carried away from their original situation by the regularity of the drift of ice to the south-westward. The life of the mariner is one always of great labour and peril, but in navigating these arctic seas he is exposed to sudden and peculiar dangers.

It is possible that the title and contents of this volume may allure to its perusal some who look forward to exposure to dangers such as those which are here described. They surely will not deem it intrusive to be reminded that the most important preparation for such undertakings, as well as for the whole of life, is to surrender the heart to that Saviour who has died to redeem his servants from guilt and ruin. The pardon and peace which he freely confers on all who come to him, are the only safe comforts of a departing soul. It is his blood only that cleanses from all sin; it is his Spirit that renews and sanctifies the mind; and whatever pain or accident may befal the body, there can be "no condemnation" in time or in eternity "to them which are in Christ Jesus." The message of God to man is the offer of a free salvation, through the death of his glorious Son. This offer must determine the eternal condition of all to whom it is in God's mercy revealed. "God so loved the world, that he gave his only begotten Son, that whosoever believeth in him should not perish, but have everlasting life!" Reader, do you understand, and have you accepted, this gracious message?

FOOTNOTES:

[1] Now sir John Ross and sir Edward Parry.

CHAPTER IV.

OBSERVATIONS ON THE ATMOSPHEROLOGY OF THE ARCTIC REGIONS, PARTICULARLY RELATING TO SPITZBERGEN AND THE ADJACENT GREENLAND SEA.

In treating of the subject of this chapter, our remarks shall, in the first instance, relate to the *climate of the Arctic Regions and the general effects of cold*. In the autumn and spring seasons, the climate of Spitzbergen and its adjacent sea is variable and tempestuous. The temperature passes through its extreme range, which, probably, exceeds fifty degrees in the same season, or even in the same month, with a rapidity unknown in countries situate within the temperate zones. North, west, and east winds bring with them the extreme cold of the icy regions immediately surrounding the Pole, whilst a shift of wind to the south-west, south, or south-east, elevates the temperature towards that of the neighbouring seas.

An arctic winter consists of the accumulation of almost everything among atmospheric phenomena that is disagreeable to the feelings, together with the privation of those bounties of Heaven with which other parts of the earth, in happier climates, are so plentifully supplied. During the whole of the winter months, the cheering rays of the sun are neither seen nor felt, and there are occasional storms of wind and snow.

The most severe cold, says Crantz, that occurs in Greenland, sets in, as in temperate climates, "after the new year; and is so piercing in February and March, that the stones split in twain, and the sea reeks like an oven." On the return of the sun, the months of May, June, and August, are even occasionally pleasant; but with July, and partially with June and August, the densest fogs prevail, which are more depressing to the spirits than even intense cold.

The temperature of the atmosphere, when the fogs prevail, is generally near the freezing point, and is not above three or four degrees higher at midday than at midnight, and sometimes does not vary above a degree or two for several days together. But, in the spring and winter seasons, the temperature is subject to very great and rapid alterations, which are frequently simultaneous with the greatest changes of pressure. This renders the thermometer a valuable appendage in the prognostication of the weather.

The great depression of temperature which takes place in the proximity of ice with a northerly wind, appears equally as considerable to the feelings in low as in high latitudes. As great a degree of cold as ever I noticed in a series of twelve years' observations (once excepted) was in latitude $71\frac{1}{4}°$, April 12, 1814, when the mean of three thermometers indicated zero; and, on the same occasion, during an interval of three days, the mean temperature was less than 5°. The wind in the mean time was continually blowing from the north-eastward, generally blowing a gale, but sometimes moderate. On the 25th of April, 1813, in latitude 8°, the thermometer fell to 4°, during a hard gale from the north-east, but on account of the ship being driven away from the ice it soon rose to 10° or 15°. The effect of the ice in reducing the temperature is so considerable, that our proximity to it is often announced by the coldness before it can be seen. In this manner, the difference of a few leagues in position sometimes produces a surprising increase of cold.

The Greenland sailors, being well defended from external cold by a choice selection of warm clothing, generally support the lowest temperature, after a few days' habitude, without much inconvenience. When, however, its attacks are not gradual, as when a ship, which has attained the edge of the ice, under a southerly gale, is exposed suddenly to a northerly breeze, the change of temperature is so great and rapid, that the most hardy cannot conceal their uneasiness under its first impression. On one occasion, in the year 1814, there was between the time of my leaving the deck at night and arising the following morning an increase in the cold of about 20°. This remarkable change was attended with singular effects. The circulation of the blood was accelerated, a sense of parched dryness was excited in the nose; the mouth, or rather lips, were contracted in all their dimensions, as by a sphincter, and the articulation of many words was rendered difficult and imperfect; indeed, every part of the body was more or less stimulated or disordered by the severity of the cold. The hands, if exposed, would have been frozen in a few minutes, and even the face could not have resisted the effects of a brisk wind, continued for any length of time. A piece of metal, when applied to the tongue, instantly adhered to it, and could not be removed without its retaining a portion of the skin; iron became brittle, and such as was at all of inferior quality might be fractured by a blow; brandy, of English manufacture and wholesale strength, was frozen; quicksilver, by a single process, might have been consolidated; the sea, in some places, was in the act of freezing, and, in others, appeared to smoke, and produced, in the formation of *frost-rime*, an obscurity greater than that of the thickest fog.

The subtle principle of magnetism seemed to be, in some way or other, influenced by the frost, for the deck compasses became sluggish, or even motionless, while a cabin compass traversed with celerity. The ship became enveloped in ice; the bows, sides, and lower rigging, were loaded; and the rudder, if not repeatedly freed, would, in a short time, have been rendered immovable. A considerable swell at this time prevailing, the smoke in the cabin, with the doors closed, was so intolerable, that we were under the necessity of giving free admission to the external air to prevent it. The consequence was, that, in front of a brisk fire, at the distance of a yard and a half from it, the temperature was 25°; water spilt on the table froze, and, indeed, congelation took place in one situation at the distance of only two feet from the stove. Hoar-frost, also, appeared in the sailors' bed-cabins, arising from their breath, and was deposited upon their blankets.

Under such a temperature, the whale-fishery could not be prosecuted, for nature could not sustain continued exposure to the pungent force of the wind. With a calm atmosphere, however, the sensible effects of cold are singularly diminished; the cold of zero then becomes equally supportable with the temperature of 10, 15, or even 20 degrees, when impressed by a brisk wind; hence, the sensations produced on the body become a very equivocal criterion for estimating the degree of cold.

The effect of cold in preventing the traversing of compasses, exposed to its influence, has been noticed by some navigators. As a remedy against this inconvenience, Ellis, in his voyage to Hudson's Bay, suggests the propriety of removing the compasses into a warm place, by which the needles speedily resume their activity. I have found, by experiments, that neither the attractive nor directive power of the magnet suffers diminution by an increase of cold. There appears, however, to be an increase of friction, or the introduction of some unknown principle, which, when the degree of cold is very much increased, occasions a diminution in the mobility of magnetic needles.

Many remarkable effects of cold are related in the journals of Polar navigators. Captain James, when wintering in Hudson's Bay, latitude 52° north, experienced such cold, that, on the 10th December, many of the sailors had their noses, cheeks, and fingers, frozen as white as paper. Ellis, who wintered in the same region, latitude 57° 30', found, by the 3rd of November, bottled beer, though wrapped in tow, and placed near a good, constant fire, frozen solid. Many of the sailors had their faces, ears, and toes frozen; iron adhered to their fingers; glasses used in drinking stuck to the mouth, and sometimes removed the skin from the lips or tongue; and a sailor, who inadvertently used his finger for stopping a spirit-bottle in place of a cork, while removing it from the house to his tent, had his finger fast frozen in the bottle, in consequence of which a part of it was obliged to be taken off to prevent mortification.

A Hamburgh whaler, beset by the ice, near Spitzbergen, in the year 1769, was exposed to great danger. The effect of the frost was such, that the seams in the ship's sides cracked with a noise resembling the report of a pistol. These openings at first rendered the vessel very leaky, but after she got free from the ice, and into a milder climate, they again closed.

In the interesting narrative, by Pelham, of the preservation of eight seamen, who were accidentally left in Spitzbergen, in the year 1630, and wintered there, are some remarks on the effects of cold. The sea of the bay, where they took up their abode, froze over on the 10th of October. After the commencement of the new year, the frost became most intense; it raised blisters in their flesh as if they had been burned with fire, and if they touched iron at such times it would stick to their fingers like bird-lime. Sometimes, when they went out of doors to procure water, they were seized in such a way by the cold, that their flesh felt as sore as if they had been cruelly beaten.

The effects of cold at Disco, as observed by M. Paul Egedé, on the 7th January, 1738, and recorded by David Crantz, in his History of Greenland, are too striking to be omitted. "The ice and hoar-frost," says Egedé, "reach through the chimney to the stove's mouth, without being thawed by the fire in the day-time. Over the chimney is an arch of frost, with little holes, through which the smoke discharges itself. The doors and walls are as if they were plastered over with frost, and, which is scarcely credible, beds are often frozen to the bedsteads. The linen is frozen in the drawers, the upper eider-down bed and the pillows are quite stiff with frost an inch thick, from the breath."

The terrific power of these mighty agencies of nature illustrate His perfections, who has all resources at his command, to minister to the comfort of his servants, or the inevitable destruction of his enemies. To be hostile to the God of heaven and of earth, is surely the height of folly as well as of ingratitude. "He sendeth forth his commandment upon earth: his word runneth very swiftly. He giveth snow like wool: he scattereth the hoar-frost like ashes. He casteth forth his ice like morsels: who can stand before his cold?"

In these frigid regions, the scurvy becomes a very alarming disease, and many individuals have perished by it, who have attempted to winter in Spitzbergen and neighbouring countries. It appears, however, probable, that this disease is not so much influenced by the severity of the climate as by the use of improper aliment. An excellent paper on this subject, by Dr. John Aikin, is published in the Memoirs of the Literary and Philosophical Society of Manchester. It affirms, that by the constant use of fresh provisions, the occasional use of oleaginous substances, together with frequent exercise, a warm dwelling, and a warm clothing, there would, probably, be little danger in exposure to the severities of a Spitzbergen winter. Whenever I have had occasion to expose myself to severe cold, I have found that the more I am heated the longer I can resist the cold without inconvenience. The warmth produced by simple fluids, such as tea or soup, is preferable to that occasioned by spirits. After the liberal use of tea, I have often sustained a cold ten degrees at the mast-head for several hours without uneasiness. I have frequently gone from the breakfast-table, where the temperature was 50° or 60°, to the mast-head, where it was ten, without any other additional clothing except a cap, yet I never received any injury, and seldom much inconvenience, from the uncommon transition.

The antiseptical property of frost is remarkable. Animal substances requisite as food, of all descriptions, (fish excepted,) may be taken to Greenland, and there preserved any length of time, without being smoked, dried, or salted. Beef, mutton, pork, and fowls, the latter neither plucked nor drawn, are constantly taken out from England, Shetland, or Orkney, and preserved in this way. When used, the beef is best divided by a saw; it is then thawed in cold water, and, if cooked, when three, four, or five months old, will frequently appear as profuse of gravy as if it had been recently killed. A further antiseptical effect is produced by the cold on animal and vegetable substances, so as to preserve them, if they remain in the same climate, unchanged for a period of many years. An instance corroborative of this remark is given by M. Bleau, who, in his Atlas Historique, informs us, that the bodies of seven Dutch seamen, who perished in Spitzbergen, in the year 1635, were found twenty years afterwards by some sailors, who happened to land about the place where they were interred, in a perfect state, not having suffered the smallest degree of putrefaction. Wood, indeed, has been met with in Spitzbergen, which has resisted all injury from the weather during the lapse of a century.

Our remarks must now be directed to *meteorology*, and to an investigation of the temperature of the north Polar regions, and its constant tendency to equalization.

Though in a state of rapid improvement, the science of meteorology is acknowledged to be yet in its infancy. Before the discovery of the weight of the atmosphere by Torricelli, about the year 1630, no means of registering its variations of pressure could be known or practised. Hence we can have no very correct idea of the relative temperature of climates in the present and remote periods, unless from occasional historical remarks of the formation of ice in particular lakes, rivers, or parts of the sea, or from the capability of the earth for producing certain fruits or grain. In consequence, however, of the use of the thermometer and barometer, meteorology, as a science, has made considerable advancement. The records of phenomena, which these instruments indicate, have proved highly useful. Professor Mayer has given us a formula for determining the temperature of any situation on the globe, where observations have not been made. Dr. Hutton has presented us with an ingenious and plausible theory of rain; and Kirwan, Humboldt, and others, have advanced our knowledge of the climates of different countries. Dr. Wells has investigated the phenomena of dew, and professor Leslie has conducted profound researches on the relations of air to heat and moisture, and on the propagation of heat and cold through the atmosphere to distant regions. By the invention, also, of several curious and useful instruments, especially the hygrometer for the measurement of the dryness or dampness of the atmosphere, he has contributed very largely to the advancement of meteorological knowledge.

The temperature of the atmosphere in any particular region is one of those phenomena, which, however they may fluctuate, or whatever may be their daily, monthly, or yearly variations, and however unequal and capricious these may be, will, on the average of numerous corresponding periods, be found to be dependent on certain laws tending to produce equilibrium; so that the general results are remarkably uniform. When we experience particularly cold winters, or particularly hot summers, we might suppose that the mean temperature of the years in which the former occur, would be greatly below, and that of years in which the hot summers occur, would be greatly above, the general standard. But this will seldom be found to be the case. In temperate climates of the northern hemisphere, the mean temperature of any one year, derived from the mean of the daily extremes of heat and cold, or from any particular number of daily observations, continued through the course of twelve successive months, seldom differs from the general mean temperature, as derived from the observation of a great, number of years, more than two or three degrees. The mean temperature of any single month cannot be supposed to be equally uniform; this, however, does not differ so widely from the general mean of the month as might be expected.

As the mean annual temperature of a country is, therefore, probably given by one year's observations only, to within two or three degrees of the truth, the mean of a period of eight or ten years will, probably, come within one degree of the truth. By the comparison of the results of thermometrical observations, made in different countries, with each other, tracing the changes of temperature, which appear with certain changes of latitude or situation, some ingenious and philosophical men have endeavoured, by principles of analogy and induction, to determine the mean temperature of every parallel of latitude from the Equator to the north Pole. These calculations have been considered as near approximations; and, as long as observations were wanting, served for purposes of investigation, to complete the scale of the temperature of the globe. When we reach, however, the regions of perpetual ice, a remarkable anomaly is discovered, the mean temperature falling below the estimation in these tables at once 17°. From a series of observations on the temperature, etc., of the Polar regions, conducted with care during twelve successive voyages to the Greenland Seas, I am able to deduce the following conclusions.

The mean temperature of the months of April, May, June, and July, are satisfactorily derived from the means of the latitudes and of the observations of temperature; but the mean temperature of the whole year, and of the winter months, wherein no observations in such high latitudes have yet been made, can only be ascertained by analogy. From the examination of numerous thermometrical registers, particularly one consisting of 54,750 observations, made in a succession of fifty years, at Stockholm, it would seem that the temperature of the year in northern latitudes is indicated by that of the 27th to 28th of April. I have collated 656 observations, made on 242 days, in nine different years, extending equally before and after the 27th of April, from which the mean temperature of the year, in latitude 76° 45', near the meridian of London, appears to be 18° 86'. Reducing all the monthly temperatures derived from my observations to the parallel of latitude 78° north, by the application of Mayer's formula, and allowing for the fact that many of the observations of April were made at a considerable distance from the ice, I calculate the temperature of April, latitude 78°, to be 14° 23', and the mean of the year in the same proportion exactly 17°. Having discovered, by observation chiefly, the mean temperature of the months of April, May, June, and July, and the probable mean temperature of the year in the icy regions adjoining Spitzbergen, I conceive it not difficult to calculate the temperature of the remaining months. The difference between the mean temperature of the year and that of July, is 21½° in Stockholm, and 20° near Spitzbergen. Finding not only that the difference of temperature between the mean of the year and July, near Spitzbergen, but that the progressive increase of temperature from April to July, also, bore a strong analogy to the relative circumstances at Stockholm, I formed a scheme of decimals, connected with a simple formula, by which the same proportion of change, which has been observed to take place every month at Stockholm, may be made very readily to apply to any other country, whence, situations and circumstances being nearly similar, the temperature of unobserved months may be calculated. The temperature of January, latitude 78°, comes out—1°; that of February, 0° 7'; March, 6° 1'; August, 34° 9'; September, 27° 8'; October, 18° 5'; November, 9° 8'; and December, 3° 1'.

Following the example of every generalizing meteorologist, I may, with some propriety, extend my observations to the probable temperature of the north Pole, provided I can proceed on data, not merely arbitrary or fanciful, but founded on observation and analogy.

It has been observed, that professor Mayer's theory for ascertaining the temperature of every latitude, becomes exceedingly wide of the truth when we approach the regions of perpetual ice, notwithstanding in most other situations on the sea, or bordering thereon, it holds sufficiently near. According to it, the mean temperature of latitude 76° 45', near the western coast of Spitzbergen, would have been 33° 8', instead of 18° 8', as shown by my observations; and, according to it, the mean temperature of the Pole is reckoned to be about 31°. The 15° difference between the observation and calculation must be considered as the frigorific effect of the ice, of which, if we can ascertain the probable measurement at the Pole, we shall be able to modify Mayer's calculation, so as to approximate to the mean temperature. At the Pole, no wind could convey the mild influence of a temperate climate, because, from whatever direction it should blow, it must be cooled down by brushing over an extensive surface of ice; consequently, the full frigorific effect of the ice must be greater in the Pole than in places situated at or near the borders of the ice. In a total period of 242 days, the temperature of the air was, by observation, found to be more or less influenced by the ice during 173 days of that period. Hence, as 173 is to 15°, the anomaly occasioned by the mean temperature, so is 242 to 21°, which is the probable anomaly that may be expected when the temperature is always influenced by the ice, or the anomaly which may be supposed to occur at the Pole. Now, if we deduct 21° from 31°, the calculated temperature of the Pole, the actual mean temperature at the Pole will be about 10°.

Concerning the pressure of the atmosphere in Polar latitudes, I would remark, particularly in the winter and spring months, it is liable to sudden and very considerable variations, and a careful study and observation of these is necessary to enable the watchful mariners to anticipate the approach of storms.

The following are the relations which, in Polar latitudes, I have been enabled to trace between the barometer and the weather:—

1. A hard westerly gale, with snow, occasions the greatest depression of the mercury; and a light easterly wind, with dry weather, the greatest elevation.

2. The rising of the mercury foretells the subsidence of wind or rain, a change of wind or fine weather; and its falling, rain, snow, or a change or increase of wind.

3. The mercury rising unusually high, and then becoming stationary, indicates, in the months of April and May, a continuance of fine weather; but in June or July, foggy weather.

4. If, in the month of April, the mercury fall with some rapidity an inch or more, a storm will most certainly succeed, however contrary appearances may be, which will probably be the more severe in proportion as it approximates the east, and will frequently continue, with unabated violence, for fifty or sixty hours.

5. The rising of the mercury usually precedes the cessation of a storm, but does not invariably determine the period of its continuance, as storms frequently blow for a day or two after the first rise of the mercury.

6. Sudden and repeated fluctuations are indicative of unsettled weather; but the rapid fall of the mercury is no indication of a short gale, though, in other regions, the reverse is said to be the case; for, before storms that continue two or three days, the barometer frequently falls an inch within twenty-four hours; and indeed, in a gale as long and as heavy as I almost ever witnessed, the fall of the mercury was above an inch in twelve hours.

7. Before very heavy storms, when the barometer falls uncommonly low, the mercury seems to get below its natural level, and often rises two or three tenths of an inch as soon as the predicted storm commences; hence this first rise of the mercury is no indication whatever of an abatement of the wind.

8. On account of the different states of the barometer in west and east winds, the usual level of the mercury, with a moderate wind at west, not being much higher than with a gale at east, a change of wind from one of these quarters to the opposite may be accompanied with the greatest alteration in the strength of the wind, without producing any effect on the barometer.

The appearance of the Greenland atmosphere corresponds in some degree with the winter sky of Britain; the colour of the former is, however, of a deeper azure, and its transparency, when clear and free from icy crystals, perhaps more perfect.

Far within the borders of compact ice the atmosphere, in summer, is often cloudless, and the weather serenely pleasant, though cold. But in the usual fishing-stations, and on the exterior of the ice in general, a clear sky is not frequent; nevertheless, when it does occur, its transparency is peculiarly beautiful. The sun sometimes sweeps two or three times round the Pole, without being for a moment obscured by a cloud. Objects the most remote may be seen perfectly distinct and clear. A ship's top-gallant-mast, at the distance of five or six leagues, may be discerned when just appearing above the horizon, with a common perspective glass; and the summits of some mountains are visible at the distance of sixty to a hundred miles. This perfect clearness occurs most frequently before easterly winds; in general, however, especially in very cold weather, objects on the horizon, when viewed with a high magnifier, appear affected with a perpetual tremor; whence the contemplation of distant objects is accomplished as perfectly with a good pocket-glass as with the best telescope. This tremulous motion is evidently produced by the quantity of delicate icy crystals which, in very low temperatures, are almost always seen floating in the air.

The general obscurity of the atmosphere, arising from clouds or fogs, is such, that the sun is frequently invisible during several successive days. At such times, when the sun is near the northern tropic, there is scarcely any sensible variation in the quantity of light from noon to midnight. Hence, when the sailors have been long abroad in the boats, or so fully engaged as to be unable to mark the progress of time, the inquiry, whether it be day or night, is not unfrequent.

There is nothing remarkable in the appearance of the sun at midnight, excepting that, when its altitude is very small, it may be viewed with the naked eye, without producing any painful sensation; but when it is more than four or five degrees above the horizon, it generally appears as effulgent as with the same elevation in Britain. The force of the sun's rays is sometimes remarkable. Where they fall upon the snow-clad surface of the ice or land, they are, in a great measure, reflected, without producing any material elevation of temperature; but when they impinge on the black exterior of a ship, the pitch on one side occasionally becomes fluid, while ice is rapidly generated on the other; or, while a thermometer, placed against the black paint-work on which the sun shines, indicates a temperature of 80° or 90°, or even more, on the opposite side of the ship a cold of 20° is sometimes found to prevail.

This remarkable force of the sun's rays is accompanied with a corresponding intensity of light. A person placed in the centre of a field or other compact body of ice, under a cloudless atmosphere and elevated sun, experiences such an extraordinary intensity of light, that if it be encountered for any length of time, is not only productive of a most painful sensation in the eyes, but sometimes of temporary, or even, as I have heard, of permanent blindness. Under such circumstances, the use of green glasses affords a most agreeable relief. Some of the Indians of North America defend their eyes by the use of a kind of wooden spectacles, having, instead of glasses, a narrow perpendicular slit opposite to each eye. This simple contrivance, which intercepts, perhaps, nine-tenths of the light that would reach a naked eye, prevents any painful consequences in the most intense reflection of light that ever occurs.

The constant light of the sun during the summer prevents the stars from being seen; and this, together with the frequency of cloudy or foggy weather, rarely admits a sight of the moon. Hence, the longitude, which is of such essential importance in navigation, can seldom be determined by lunar observations. Chronometers, therefore, though but little used by the whale-fishers, become of enhanced value; and even a good watch, well regulated, will, where the degrees of longitude are so very contracted, point out the meridianal situation of the ship for short intervals, with a very tolerable degree of accuracy.

Though the air in the arctic seas is generally in a state of dampness, approaching to complete saturation, yet the absolute quantity of moisture cannot, when the cold is very excessive, be considerable. It is remarked, that vessels are less apt to rust here than in any other climate; and this observation, if we consider the relative humidity of the atmosphere as indicated by the hygrometer, is certainly correct; but though the air in the Polar regions is generally damp, yet it is probable there is no habitable situation in the known world in which such a degree of actual dryness prevails, as in a house or in the cabin of a ship, well heated, when the external air is intensely cold. The wainscoting of the cabin of a ship in cold weather sometimes shrinks, in consequence of the uncommon dryness, as much as half an inch in a panel of about fifteen inches broad, being equal to one-thirtieth of the breadth; but, on returning to Britain, the same panel expands again to almost its original dimensions.

Few observations, comparatively, seem to have been made on the electricity of the atmosphere, especially in high latitudes. Perhaps, some trials that I made in the spring of 1818, on this subject, were the first that have been attempted within the arctic circle. When in latitude 68°, I erected an insulated conductor, eight feet above the maintop-gallant mast-head, connected by a copper wire with a copper ball, attached by a silk string to the deck. The conductor consisted of a slender tapering tube of tinned iron, terminated by a pointed brass wire. It was fixed in an iron socket, supported by a large cylindrical piece of glass; which glass, by means of another iron socket, was secured to the top of a long pole, elevated several feet above the mast-head. A tin cone encompassed the bottom of the conductor, the mouth of which being downward, defended the rod of glass from getting wet, so as to injure its insulated property. The conducting wire, being kept clear of the rigging of the ship, was expected to exhibit in the ball, where it terminated, any difference between the state of the electricity of the ship or sea and that of the atmosphere. The test of electricity was a Bennet's gold-leaf electrometer, brought into contact with the ball; but though trials were made for several successive days, from lat. 78° to lat. 75°, during clear, cloudy, and showery weather, not the least excitation was ever observed. That the effect might be rendered more perceptible, the electrometer was well dried and warmed immediately before each experiment, without which, indeed, no excitation could be produced in it, either with glass or sealing-wax. The nights being light, the aurora borealis could not be seen; but on the evening of the 20th of May, an appearance was observed, very much resembling the aurora borealis, yet no signs of electricity were observed in the electrometer applied to the conductor.

There are several phenomena of the atmosphere dependent on reflection and refraction, deserving of notice. *Ice-blinks* have been already mentioned, when speaking of the ice. Under certain circumstances, all objects seen on the horizon seem to be lifted above it a distance of two to four, or more, minutes of altitude, or so far extended in height above their natural dimensions. Ice, land, ships, boats, and other objects, when thus enlarged and elevated, are said to *loom*. The lower part of *looming* objects are sometimes connected with the sensible horizon by an apparent fibrous or columnar extension of their parts, which columns are always perpendicular to the horizon; at other times, they appear to be quite lifted into the air, a void space being seen between them and the horizon. This phenomenon is observed most frequently on, or before, an easterly wind, and is generally considered as indicative of such.

A most extraordinary appearance of the Foreland, or Charles's Island, Spitzbergen, occurred on the 16th of July, 1814. While sailing to the southward, along the coast, with an easterly wind, I observed what appeared to be a mountain, in the form of a slender, but elevated, monument. I was surprised that I had never seen it before, and was more astonished when I saw, not far distant, a prodigious and perfect arch thrown across a valley, of above a league in breadth. The neighbouring mountains disclosed the cause, by exhibiting an unnatural elevation with the columnar structure of looming objects. Presently, the scene was changed, the mountains along the whole coast assumed the most fantastical forms; the appearance of castles, with lofty spires, towers, and battlements, would, in a few minutes, be converted into a vast arch or romantic bridge. These varied, and sometimes beautiful, metamorphoses naturally suggested the reality of fairy descriptions; for the air was perfectly transparent; the contrast of snow and rocks was quite distinct; even in the substance of the most uncommon phantasms, though examined with a powerful telescope, and every object deemed to possess every possible stability. I never before observed a phenomenon so varied or so amusing. The land was not alone affected by this peculiar refraction, since every object between the north-east and south-east points of the compass was, more or less, deformed by it. A mass of ice on the horizon appeared of the height of a cliff, and the prismatic structure of its front suggested the idea of basaltic columns. It may be remarked, that these phenomena took place on a clear evening, after an uncommonly warm afternoon.

I observed many other peculiar effects of refraction. Such phenomena are frequent on the commencement or approach of easterly winds, and are probably occasioned by the commixture, near the surface of the land or sea, of two streams of air of different temperatures, so as to occasion an irregular deposition of imperfectly condensed vapour, which, when passing the verge of the horizon, produced these appearances.

Parhelia, mock suns, and *corona*, haloes, are perhaps not so frequent in Greenland as in some parts of America. I do not recollect to have observed them more than thrice. In the first instance, I did not minutely notice the particulars. I recollect, however, there were two or three parhelia, and four or five coloured circles, some of which almost equalled in their colours the brilliancy of the rainbow. On the second occasion, several parhelia were succeeded by a lunar halo, together with the aurora borealis, and proved the harbingers of a tremendous tempest. The last phenomenon of the kind which I saw, consisted of a large circle of luminous whiteness, passing through the centre of the sun, in a direction nearly parallel with the horizon, intersected in various places with coloured circles of smaller dimensions.

Rainbows are common in these regions, but the *fog-bow*, or *fog-circle*, is more rarely observed, and is entitled to our attention. It is a circle depicted on the fog, which prevails in the Polar seas, at certain seasons, resting upon the surface of the water, and seldom reaching to a considerable height. On the 19th July, 1813, I observed one of about 30° diameter, with bands of vivid colours depicted on the fog. The centre of the circle was in a line drawn from the sun, through the point of vision, until it met the visible vapour in a situation exactly opposite to the sun. The lower part of the circle descended beneath my feet to the side of the ship, and although it could not be a hundred feet from the eye, it was perfect, and the colours distinct. The centre of the coloured circle was distinguished by my own shadow, the head of which, enveloped by a halo, was most conspicuously portrayed. I remained a long time contemplating the beautiful phenomenon before me.

In the phenomena of the winds, which I am now about to describe, I cannot be so precise as I have been in my observations on atmospheric temperature and pressure; being able to give a correct idea only of their peculiarities and direction, whilst their relative force, founded on conjecture, I am unable to express otherwise than in the phraseology of the mariner, which, it must be allowed, is somewhat ambiguous.

In proportion as we recede from the equator, we find the winds become more variable, irregular, and partial. Storms and calms, in the northern regions, repeatedly alternate, without warning or progression; forcible winds blow at one place, when, at the distance of a few leagues, gentle breezes prevail; a storm from the south, on one hand, exhausts its impetuosity upon the gentle breeze, blowing from off the ice on the other, without prevailing in the least; ships, within the circle of the horizon, may be seen enduring every variety of wind and weather at the same moment; come becalmed, and tossing about by the violence of the waves; some, under close-reefed topsails, labouring under the force of a storm; and others, flying under gentle breezes, from quarters as diverse as the cardinal points.

The most general preliminaries to *sudden storms* are perfect calms; curiously variable breezes, with strong squalls; singular agitation of the sea, together with thick snow, which often changes from flakes to powder, and falls in such profusion, as to occasion an astonishing gloominess and obscurity in the atmosphere. If the snow clear away, the gale is often at hand, whilst a luminousness on the horizon, resembling the ice-blink, sometimes points out its direction, and a noise in the upper regions of the air announces its immediate approach. In this variable and occasionally tempestuous climate, the value of the barometer is satisfactorily proved. My father once removed his ship from a most dangerous bight in the main ice, where she would probably have been lost, had she remained a few moments longer, in consequence of his having heard the rushing of a storm in the air, while at the mast-head. Before the ship was out of danger, a heavy gale commenced, but the sails being set, and the ship under command, she was extricated from the perilous situation. From this circumstance, he imagined that sudden storms frequently commence at some height in the atmosphere, and gradually descend to the surface. *Intermitting gales* are almost equally common with sudden storms, and variable winds prevail, in an extraordinary degree, in the frigid zone. The winds, indeed, among ice, are generally unsteady in their direction, and attended with strong gusts or squalls, particularly in very cold weather, and towards the termination of a storm. This variableness, being the effect of the unequal temperature of the ice and water, is curious, but the phenomenon that is most calculated to excite surprise is, that several distinct, and even opposite winds, with the force, in many instances, of a fresh gale, will occasionally prevail at the same moment of time, within the range of the horizon. The situation in which this circumstance occurs, would appear to be the point where conflicting winds contend for the superiority; and as, in some instances, their forces are effectually balanced, the winds, which simultaneously blow from the southward and northward, or from the eastward and westward, have their energies almost destroyed at the place of combination. Thus it sometimes happens that ships, within sight of each other, will, at the same period of time, experience every variety of weather, from calm to storm, from fair weather to thickest snow, together with several distinct and contrary currents of wind.

On the morning of the 30th of April, 1810, the ship Resolution—in which I served in the capacity of chief-mate, or harpooner—was, during thick showers of snow, sailing by the edge of a stream of ice, with the wind from the north-westward. About ten, A. M., the snow abated, and several ships were seen within the distance of three or four miles. As all of these ships were sailing "on a wind," it was easy to ascertain the direction of the wind where they were, and curious to observe its variableness. Two ships, bearing north-east from us, had the wind at north-east; two, bearing east, had east or east-north-east; two, bearing south-east, had the wind at south-east; while, with us, it blew from the north-west. In each of these situations a fresh breeze prevailed; but in some situations, where there happened to be no ships, there appeared to be no wind at all. The clouds above us, at the time, we're constantly changing their forms. Showers of snow were seen in various places at a distance.

Instances of *local storms* are not uncommon in temperate climates, but in the arctic regions they are frequent and striking. Their locality is such, that a calm may occur when a storm is expected and actually does prevail at a short distance, so that the indication of the barometer may appear to be erroneous. In such cases, however, the reality of the storm is often proved by the agitation of the sea. Swells from various quarters make their appearance, and frequently prevail at the same time. My father, whose opportunities of observation have been very numerous, relates the following instance of the locality of a storm. When commanding the ship Henrietta, he was on one occasion navigating the Greenland Sea during a tedious gale of wind, accompanied with snowy weather. As the wind began to abate, a ship appeared in sight, under all sails, and presently came up with the Henrietta. The master hailed, and inquired what had happened that my father's ship was under close-reefed top-sail in such moderate weather. On being told that a storm had just subsided, he declared that he knew nothing of it; he observed, indeed, a swell, and noticed a black cloud a-head of his ship that seemed to advance before him until he was overshadowed with it a little while before he overtook the Henrietta, but he had had fine weather and light winds the whole day!

A single instance is given of those sudden gusts and various currents of wind, which occur at some elevation in the atmosphere, and which are common to all climates. On a particularly fine day, my father having landed on the northern part of Charles's island, incited by the same curiosity which led him on shore, ascended, though not without great difficulty and fatigue, a considerable elevation, the summit of which was not broader than a common table, and which shelved on one side as steep as the roof of a house, and on the other formed a mural precipice. Engaged in admiring the extensive prospect from an eminence of about two thousand feet, he scarcely noticed the advance of a very small cloud. Its rapid approach and peculiar form (having somewhat the appearance of a hand) at length excited his attention, and when it reached the place where he was seated in a calm air, a torrent of wind assailed him with such violence, that he was obliged to throw himself on his body and stick his hands and feet in the snow to prevent himself from being hurled over the tremendous slope which threatened his instant destruction. The cloud having passed, the air, to his great satisfaction, became calm, when he immediately descended by sliding down the surface of snow, and in a few minutes reached the base of the mountain in safety.

The course of the seasons, as relates to prevailing winds, is as follows. In the spring months, north-east and east winds are frequent, with severe storms from these and other quarters. The storms from the north-east, east, and south-east, are generally the most violent. When they occur in March and April, they frequently continue without intermission for two or three successive days, and rarely subside till the wind veers round to the north or north-west. Storms, in the spring of the year, blowing from the south-east, generally change, before they abate, to the east, north-east, north, and north-west; but storms commencing at south-west or south, usually veer, before they subside, in the contrary direction, towards the north-west, and sometimes continue changing until their strength is spent in the north or north-east quarter. A storm beginning to blow from the western quarter seldom continues long; when it blows hard it commonly veers to the north or north-east, and it is observable that a very hard southerly or easterly gale is frequently succeeded within a few days by another from the opposite quarter. With the advance of the month of May, storms become less frequent, and the weather becomes sensibly better. The winds then begin to blow more frequently from the north-west; in June, the most common winds are north and north-west, south and south-west; and in July, south and south-westerly winds prevail. At this season, calms or very light winds also become frequent, and continue sometimes for several days together. In high northern latitudes, however, very heavy storms from the southward occur in July, and blow for thirty or forty hours at a time. In August, north-east winds begin again to prevail. The south-west and southerly storms of the autumn blow with particular violence. "The wind rages so vehemently, that the houses quiver and crack, the tents and lighter boats fly up in the air, and the sea-water scatters about in the land like snow-dust—nay, the Greenlanders say that the storm rends off stones a couple of pounds' weight, and mounts them in the air. In summer, whirlwinds also spring up, that draw up the waters out of the sea, and turn a boat round several times."

When the countries of temperate climates suffer under tempests in frequent succession, Polar regions enjoy comparative tranquillity. After the autumn gales have passed, a series of calm weather, attended by severe frosts, frequently succeeds. So striking, indeed, is the stillness of the northern winter, that there is truth in Dr. Guthrie's observation, that nature seems "to have studied perfect equality in the distribution of her favours, as it is only parts of the earth which most enjoy the kindly influences of the sun that suffer by the effects of its superior heat, so that if the atmosphere of the north is not so genial as that of the south, at least it remains perfectly quiet and serene, without threatening destruction to man and the product of his industry as in what are called happier climates."

The principal meteors, not being of the aqueous kind, that remain to be considered are lightning and the aurora borealis. As we approach the Pole, the former phenomenon becomes more rare, and the latter more common. Lightning, indeed, is seldom seen to the northward of the arctic circle, and when it does occur, it is very seldom accompanied by thunder.

In Spitzbergen, neither thunder nor lightning has, I believe, ever been observed. For my own part, I have never seen lightning northward of latitude 65°, and only in two instances when at any considerable distance from land. The aurora borealis occurs independent of land and of cold, becoming more frequent in its appearance as we approach the Pole, and enlivening by its brilliancy and peculiar grandeur the tedious gloom of the long winter nights. Its appearance, though not very frequently seen in Britain, is very common as far south as Shetland and Feroe. In Iceland, and other countries bordering on the arctic circle, the northern lights occur almost every clear night during the winter. In the summer, they can seldom be seen on account of the presence of the sun, and in the spring of the year, the obscurity of the atmosphere prevents their frequent exhibition. In several instances, I have known stormy weather follow the appearance of the brilliant aurora, and one of the most tremendous storms I was ever exposed to, succeeded a splendid exhibition of the northern lights. Under certain circumstances, especially when they are seen at a considerable altitude above the horizon, having a red or copper colour, they are supposed to be indicative of a violent storm.

Our chapter on atmospherical phenomena must now be concluded by observations on aqueous meteors; including clouds, rain, hail, snow, frost-rime, hoar-frost, and fog.

Very little clear weather occurs in the Greenland seas, for often when the atmosphere is free from any visible vapour on the land, at sea it is obscured by frost-rime in the spring of the year, and by clouds or fog in the summer; so that scarcely one-twentieth of the season devoted to the whale-fishery can be said to consist of clear weather.

The *clouds* most generally consist of a dense stratum of obscurity, composed of irregular compact patches covering the whole expanse of the heavens. The *cirrus*, *cirrocumulus*, and *cirrostratus*, of Howard's nomenclature, are occasionally distinct; the *nimbus* is partly formed, but never complete: and the grandeur of the *cumulus* or thunder-cloud is never seen, unless it be on the land. In the atmosphere over the coasts in Greenland and Spitzbergen, where the air is greatly warmed by the concentration and reflection of the sun's rays in the sheltered valleys, a small imperfect cumulus is sometimes exhibited.

The known agents made use of in the economy of nature for the production of rain are changes of temperature and electricity. The latter principle is supposed to act most powerfully in the production of thunder-showers, in which case it is not unlikely that a portion of the air of the atmosphere is, by the passing of the lightning from one cloud to another, converted into water. The former seems to be the chief agent in the colder regions of the globe, where electricity is either more equal in its distribution, or not so active in its operations as in the warmer climates. From the beautiful theory of the late

Dr. James Hutton, supported by the researches of professor Leslie, it appears, that "while the temperature advances uniformly in arithmetical progression, the dissolving power which this communicates to the air mounts with the accelerating rapidity of a geometrical series;" and this in such a ratio, that the "air has its dryness doubled at each rise of temperature answering to fifteen centesimal degrees," or twenty-seven of Fahrenheit. Hence, "whatever be the actual condition of a mass of air, there must always exist some temperature at which it would become perfectly damp;" and hence whenever two streams of air saturated with moisture of different temperatures are mixed together, or brush against one another, in the form of different currents of wind, there must always be a quantity of moisture precipitated. For if two masses of air, of different temperatures, but equal in quantity, and both saturated with moisture, were mixed together, the resulting temperature would be nearly the mean of the two, but, at that temperature, the capacity of air for moisture being less than the quantity contained in the two commixed masses, the surplus must be deposited.

Rain is by no means common in the Polar countries excepting in the months of July and August, and then only with southerly or westerly winds. During all seasons of the year, however, with strong gales blowing from a southern climate, rain is occasionally observed in situations near the edge of the ice; but snow or sleet are more common even under such circumstances; and in remote situations among ice, near the 80th parallel of latitude, rain seldom or never occurs.

Hail is a much more familiar meteor in temperate than in frigid climates. In the Greenland Sea, this aqueous concretion is very rarely seen; and if we define it as consisting of pellucid spheres of ice, generated in the atmosphere, it may be said to be unknown in very high latitudes. This fact is in favour of the electrical origin of hail, as it is well-known to be common in temperate climates, where the air is in a high state of electricity, and to be the frequent concomitant of thunder and lightning. The only substance resembling hail that is generated in the frigid zone consists of a white, porous, spherical concretion of light and snowy texture.

Snow is so very common in the arctic regions, that it may be boldly stated, that in nine days out of ten, in April, May, and June, more or less snow falls. With southerly winds, near the borders of the ice, or in situations where humid air, blowing from the sea, assimilates with a gelid breeze from the ice, the heaviest falls of snow occur. In this case, a depth of two or three inches is sometimes deposited in an hour. The thickest precipitations also frequently precede sudden storms. The form of the particles of snow presents an endless variety. When the temperature of the air is within a degree or two of the freezing point, much snow falls, frequently consisting of large irregular flakes, such as are common in Britain. Sometimes it exhibits small granular, or large rough white concretions; at others, it consists of white spiculæ, or rude stellated crystals. But in severe frosts, though the sky appears perfectly clear, lamellar flakes of snow, of the most regular and beautiful forms, are always seen floating in the air, and sparkling in the sunbeams, and the snow which falls in general is of most elegant texture and appearance.

Snow, of a reddish or brownish colour, is not unfrequently seen. The brownish stain, which occurs on shore, is given by an earthy substance brought from the mountains by the streams of water, derived from thawing ice and snow, or the fall of rain. The reddish colour, as far as I have observed, is given by the mute of birds; though, in the example met with by captain Ross, in Baffin's Bay, the stain appears to have been of a vegetable nature. The little auk, (*Alca alle*,) which feeds upon shrimps, is found, in some parts of the Polar seas, in immense numbers. They frequently retreat to pieces of ice, or surfaces of snow, and stain them all over red with their mute. Martens saw red snow in Spitzbergen, which he considered as being stained by rain-water running down by the rocks.

The extreme beauty and endless variety of the microscopic objects procured in the animal and vegetable kingdoms, are perhaps fully equalled, if not surpassed, in both particulars of beauty and variety, by the crystals of snow. The principal configurations are the stelliform and hexagonal, though almost every shape, of which the generating angles of 60° and 12° are susceptible, may, in the course of a few years' observation, be discovered. The various modifications of crystals may be classed under five general kinds, or genera.

1. *Lamellar*, infinite in variety, most delicate in structure, and capable of subdivision into several distinct species.

2. *A lamellar, or spherical nucleus, with spinous ramifications in different planes.* This genus also consists of two or three species.

3. *Fine spiculæ, or six-sided prisms.* The finest specimens resemble white hair, cut into lengths not exceeding a quarter of an inch.

4. *Hexagonal pyramids.* I have but once seen this kind of snow crystal.

5. *Spiculæ, or prisms having one or both extremities inserted in the centre of a lamellar crystal.* This genus resembles a pair of wheels, united by an axle-tree.

In low temperatures, the greatest proportion of crystals that fall are, probably, perfect geometrical figures.

Some of the general varieties in the figures of the crystals may be referred to the temperature of the air; but the particular and endless modifications of similar classes of crystals can only be referred to the pleasure of the great First Cause, whose works, even the most minute and evanescent, and in regions the most remote from human observation, bear the impress of His own hand, and display to his intelligent creatures his vast and beneficent wisdom. If, on these forms of unintelligent matter, he has bestowed such excellent workmanship, with how much more transcendent loveliness will he clothe those who are redeemed by the exceeding riches of his grace, and who, beyond the history and productions of all worlds, will reflect the beauty of his glorious countenance!

Frost-rime, or frost-smoke, is a meteor peculiar to those parts of the globe where a very low temperature prevails for a considerable time. It consists of a dense frozen vapour, apparently arising out of the sea, or any large sheet of water, and ascending, in high winds and turbulent seas, to the height of eighty or one hundred feet, but, in light breezes and smooth water, creeping along the surface. The particles of which it consists are as small as dust, and cleave to the rigging of ships, or almost any substance against which they are driven by the wind, and afford a coating of an inch or upwards in depth. These particles adhere to one another until the windward surface of the ropes is covered, and form long fibres somewhat of a prismatical or pyramidal shape, having their points directed towards the wind. Frost-rime adheres readily to articles of clothing; and, from the circumstance of its lodging in the hair, and giving it the appearance of being powdered, the sailors humorously style it "the barber." Such of the frost-rime as is dislodged from the rigging whenever the ship is tacked, covers the deck to a considerable thickness, and, when trod upon, emits an acute sound, resembling the crushing of fine particles of glass. The cause of this phenomenon, which generally is not observed until the cold is reduced to $14°$, may perhaps be similar to that producing rain, and may be explained according to Dr. Hutton's theory.

An aqueous vapour, consisting of very minute frozen particles, sometimes occupies the lower regions of the atmosphere in temperate and frigid climates, during frosty weather, and is deposited on the ground, on surfaces of ice, or almost any other substance with which it comes in contact. This vapour seems to be of the nature of *hoar-frost*; it generally appears in the evening, after a bright sunshiny day.

Fog, or mist, is the last meteor that remains to be considered. This is one of the greatest annoyances that the arctic whalers have to encounter. It frequently prevails during the greater part of the month of July, and sometimes, at considerable intervals, in June and August. Its density is often such, that it circumscribes the prospect to an area of a few acres, not being pervious to sight at the distance of a hundred yards. It frequently lies so low that the brightness of the sun is scarcely at all intercepted; in such cases, substances warmed by the sun's rays, give to the air immediately above them increased capacity for moisture, by which evaporation goes briskly on during the densest fogs. In Newfoundland, on occasions when the sun's rays penetrate the mist, and heat the surface of the rocks, fish is frequently dried during the thickest fogs. Fogs are more frequent and more dense at the borders of the ice than near the coast of Spitzbergen. They occur principally when the mercury, in the thermometer, is near the freezing point, but they are by no means uncommon with the temperature of 40° or 45°. They are most general with south-westerly, southerly, and south-easterly winds. They seldom occur with high winds, yet in one or two instances I have observed them very thick, even in storms. Rain generally disperses them. Fogs, by increasing the apparent distances of objects, appear sometimes to magnify men into giants, hummocks of ice into mountains, and common pieces of drift-ice into heavy floes or bergs. They are an especial annoyance to the whale-fisher, and greatly perplex the navigator, by preventing him from obtaining observations for the correction of his latitude and longitude, so that he often sails in complete uncertainty. Fogs are more common near the ice than in the vicinity of the land, more frequent in open seasons than in close seasons, and more intense and more common in the southern fishing-stations than in the most northern.

CHAPTER V.

A SKETCH OF THE ZOOLOGY OF THE ARCTIC REGIONS.

In the arrangement of the following original observations on, and descriptions of the more remarkable animals inhabiting, or frequenting, Spitzbergen and the adjacent seas, I have followed Linnæus, in combination with La Cepède. The latter author has published a most voluminous and pleasing account of cetaceous animals, and has made some judicious changes in the Linnæan arrangements. By La Cepède, for instance, whales having the dorsal fin are separated from those without it; the former being called, in distinction from the latter, *Balænopteræ*, signifying whales with a fin.

Our first description must relate to the animals of the *cetaceous kind*, which frequent the Greenland Seas.

Of these the first in eminence and of importance to our commerce, is the *Balæna mysticetus*, the common or Greenland whale. This animal is productive of more oil than any other of the cetacea, and being less active, slower in its motion, and more timid than any other of its kind, of similar, or nearly similar, magnitude, it is more easily captured. Its size has been much overrated, and, in his excellent natural history of cetaceous animals, La Cepède has been guilty of considerable exaggeration. In the age when whales were regarded with superstitious dread, it is easy to conceive that the dimensions of an animal inhabiting an element in which it cannot easily be measured, would be recorded with extravagance. Authors of the first respectability in the present day give a length of eighty to one hundred feet to the mysticetus, and remark with unqualified assertion, that when the captures were less frequent, and the animals had sufficient time to attain their full growth, specimens were found of one hundred and fifty to two hundred feet in length, or even longer; and some ancient naturalists, indeed, have gone so far as to assert, that whales had been seen of above nine hundred feet in length. In the present day, however, it is certain that they are by no means so bulky. Of three hundred and twenty-two individuals, in the capture of which I have been personally concerned, no one, I believe, exceeded sixty feet in length, and the largest I ever measured was fifty-eight feet, from one extremity to the other, being one of the largest to appearance which I ever saw. An uncommon whale that was caught near Spitzbergen, about twenty years ago, the whalebone of which measured almost fifteen feet, was not, I understand, so much as seventy feet in length; and the longest actual measurement that I have met with, or heard of, is given by sir Charles Giesecké, who informs us, that in the spring of 1813, a whale was killed at Godhaven of the length of sixty-seven feet. These, however, are very uncommon instances. I therefore conceive that sixty feet may be considered as the size of the larger animals of this species, and sixty-five feet in length as a magnitude which very rarely occurs.

I believe, too, that whales are now met with of as large dimensions as at any former period since the commencement of the whale-fishery; a point which, I think, can be established from various historical records.

The greatest circumference of the whale is from thirty to forty feet. It is thickest a little behind the fins, or in the middle, between the anterior and posterior extremes of the animal, from whence it gradually tapers in a conical form towards the tail, and slightly towards the head. Its form is cylindrical, from the neck to within ten feet of the tail, beyond which it becomes somewhat quadrangular, the greatest ridge being upward, or on the back, and running backward nearly across the middle of the tail. The head has somewhat of a triangular shape. The under-part, the arched outline of which is given by the jaw-bones, is flat, and measures sixteen to twenty feet in length, and ten to twelve in breadth. The lips, extending fifteen or twenty feet in length, and five or six in height, and forming the cavity of the mouth, are attached to the under-jaw, and rise from the jaw-bones at an angle of about 80°, having the appearance, when viewed in front, of the letter U. The upper-jaw, including the "crown-bone," or skull, is bent down at the extremity, so as to shut the front and upper parts of the cavity of the mouth, and is overlapped by the lips in a squamous manner at the sides.

When the mouth is open, it presents a cavity as large as a room, and capable of containing a merchant-ship's jolly-boat full of men, being six or eight feet wide, ten or twelve feet high in front, and fifteen or sixteen feet long. The fins, two in number, are placed between one-third and two-fifths of the length of the animal, from the snout, and about two feet behind the angle of the mouth. They are seven to nine feet in length, and four or five in breadth; and in the living animal are capable of considerable flexion. The whale has no dorsal fin.

The tail, comprising in a single surface eighty or one hundred square feet, is a formidable instrument of motion or defence. Its length is only five or six feet, but its width is eighteen to twenty-four or twenty-six feet. Its position is horizontal. In its form it is flat and semi-lunar, indented in the middle, the two lobes somewhat pointed and turned a little backward. Its motions are rapid and universal; its strength immense.

The eyes are situated in the sides of the head, about a foot obliquely above and behind the angle of the mouth. They are little larger than those of an ox. The whale has no external ear. The spiracles or nostrils of the whale are two longitudinal apertures, six or eight inches in length, from which a moist vapour, mixed with mucous, is discharged when the animal breathes, but no water accompanies it unless the breathing takes place under the surface. The mouth, in place of teeth, contains two extensive rows of "fins," or whalebone, which are suspended from the sides of the crown-bone. Each series, or side of bone, as the whale-fishers term it, consists of upwards of three hundred laminæ, of which the longest are near the middle. Ten or eleven feet is the average length, and the greatest breadth at the gum ten or twelve inches. The interior edges of these laminæ are covered with a fringe of hair. In the youngest whales, called suckers, the whalebone is only a few inches long; when the length reaches six feet or upwards, the whale is said to be of *size*. The colour of the whalebone is brownish black, or bluish black, and occasionally striped longitudinally with white. A large whale sometimes affords a ton and a half of whalebone. The gum, in which the thick ends of the whalebone are inserted, is white, fibrous, tender, and tasteless. It cuts like cheese, and has the appearance of the kernel of the cocoanut. The animal has a large tongue, a slight beard, and a remarkably narrow throat.

The milk of the whale resembles that of quadrupeds in appearance, and is said to be rich and well-flavoured. In the female, two paps are situated on the abdomen.

The colour of the mysticetus is velvet black, grey, and white, with a tinge of yellow, according to the parts of the body. The older animals contain the most grey and white; under-sized whales are altogether of a bluish black, and suckers of a pale bluish, or bluish grey colour.

The skin of the body is slightly furrowed, but on the tail it is smooth. That part of the skin, which can be pulled off in sheets after it has been dried a little in the air, or particularly in the frost, is not thicker than parchment. The *rete mucosum* in adults is about three-fourths of an inch in thickness over most parts of the body. Under it lies the true skin, white and tough, and immediately in contact with it the blubber.

This most valuable portion of the animal encompasses its whole body. Its colour is yellowish white, yellow, or red; in old animals sometimes resembling the substance of the salmon. It swims in water. Its thickness all round the body is eight or ten to twenty inches, varying in different parts, as well as in different individuals. The lips are composed almost entirely of blubber, and yield from one to two tons of pure oil each. The oil appears retained in the blubber in minute cells, connected by a strong reticulated combination of tendinous fibres, which are condensed at the surface, and appears to form the substance of the skin. The oil is expelled when heated. In its fresh state, the blubber is without unpleasant smell, and it is only at the end of the voyage that the cargo of a Greenland ship becomes disagreeable.

The quantity of oil yielded by a certain quantity of blubber varies according to the age of the animal; the blubber of the sucker contains a very small portion. The quantity of oil generally bears a proportion to the length of the longest blade of whalebone. Four tons of blubber in measure generally produce three tons of oil; the ton of oil being two hundred and fifty-two gallons, wine-measure.

The flesh of the young whale is of a red colour, and, when broiled and seasoned with pepper and salt, eats like coarse beef. The bones are very porous, and contain much fine oil. The ribs are thirteen in number, and are nearly solid, and the bones of the fins, in number and proportion, are similar to those of the fingers of the human hand.

A stout whale, of sixty feet in length, is of the enormous weight of seventy tons; the blubber weighs about thirty tons; the bones of the head, whalebone, fins, and tail, eight or ten; the carcase thirty or thirty-two.

The whale is dull of hearing, but its sense of seeing is acute, especially when under water. It has no voice, but makes in breathing or blowing a very loud noise. It blows or breathes about four or five times a minute, discharging vapour to the height of some yards, which, at a distance, looks like a puff of smoke. When the animal is wounded, this vapour is often stained with blood, and on the approach of death jets of blood are sometimes discharged. The whale being lighter than the water, can remain at the surface with ease, but requires considerable exertion to descend. It advances through the water by means of the tail, which, to attain the greatest velocity, is moved alternately upward and downward; and, for slower progress, laterally and obliquely downward, in the manner of *skulling* a boat. The fins are used for balancing the animal, and in bearing off their young. I have observed a whale descending, after I had harpooned it, to the depth of four hundred fathoms, with the average velocity of seven or eight miles per hour. The usual rate at which whales swim, however, seldom exceeds four miles an hour, and though their extreme velocity may be eight or nine, yet we find this speed never continues longer than for a few minutes. They sometimes ascend with such rapidity as to leap entirely out of the water, apparently for amusement, and to the high admiration of the distant spectator. At other times they throw themselves into a perpendicular posture, with their heads downward, and rearing their tails on high in the air, they beat the water with awful violence; the sea is thrown into foam, the air is filled with vapours, and the noise in calm weather is heard to a great distance. Sometimes the whale shakes its tremendous tail in the air, which, cracking like a whip, resounds to the distance of two or three miles.

When it retires from the surface, it first lifts its head, then plunging it under water, elevates its back, like the segment of a sphere, deliberately rounds it away towards the extremity, throws its tail out of the water, and then disappears. Whales usually remain at the surface to breathe about two minutes, during which time they "blow" eight or nine times, and then descend for an interval usually of five or ten minutes, but sometimes, when feeding, fifteen or twenty. They commonly descend to only a trifling depth; but, when struck, they have been known, by the quantity of line taken out of the boat, to descend to the depth of an English mile, and, with such velocity, as to break their jaw-bones by the blow struck against the bottom. Occasionally, they may be found sleeping in calm weather among ice, and some persons are of opinion that, when undisturbed, they can remain under the surface for many hours at a time.

The food of the whale consists of various species of *actiniæ, clioncs, sepiæ, medusæ, cancri,* and *helices,* judging from the fact that some of these genera are always to be seen wherever any tribe of whales is found stationary. I have only discovered in the stomachs of dead animals *squillæ* or shrimps. When the whale feeds, it swims swiftly through the sea, with its jaws extended; its food is entangled by the whalebone, which, from its compact arrangement and thick internal covering of hair, does not allow a particle to escape.

The whale has one young at a birth. At this time the young one is said to be at least ten feet long, and continues under the protection of the mother for probably a year, until, by the growth of the whalebone, it is able to maintain itself. It probably reaches the magnitude called *size*, that is, with a six feet length of whalebone, in twelve years, and attains its full growth at the age of twenty or twenty-five. Whales live to a great age. The maternal affection of the whale is very interesting. The cub, being insensible to danger, is easily harpooned, and is sometimes struck as a snare to secure the mother. In this case she joins it at the surface whenever it has occasion to rise for respiration, encourages it to swim off, assists its flight by taking it under her fin, and seldom deserts it while life remains. In June, 1811, one of my harpooners struck a sucker, with the hope of its leading to the capture of the mother. Presently she arose close by "the fast-boat," and seizing the young one, dragged about a hundred fathoms of line out of the boat with remarkable force and velocity. Again she rose to the surface, darted furiously to and fro, frequently stopped short, or suddenly changed her direction, and gave every possible intimation of extreme agony. For a length of time she continued thus to act, though closely pursued by the boats; and, inspired with courage and resolution by her concern for her offspring, seemed regardless of the danger which surrounded her. At length, one of the boats approached so near that a harpoon was hove at her. It hit, but did not attach itself. A second harpoon was struck, this also failed to penetrate, but a third was more effectual, and held. Still she did not attempt to escape, but allowed other boats to approach, so that, in a few minutes, three more harpoons were fastened, and, in the course of an hour afterwards she was killed.

There is something deeply interesting in the manner in which the great Maker of all things, in giving laws to the animal kingdom, has thus presented so many illustrations of the parental relation. It is as if he would not leave his intelligent creatures destitute of memorials of their relation to himself; so that, while in the field and on the flood, they behold the signs of parental affection and filial dependence, they may be led to ponder the solemn question of their tender and faithful Parent in heaven—"If, then, I be a Father, where is mine honour?"

The mysticetus occurs most abundantly in the frozen seas of Greenland and Davis's Strait, in the bays of Baffin and Hudson, in the sea to the northward of Behring's Strait, and along some part of the northern shores of Asia, and probably America. It is never met with in the German Ocean, and rarely within two hundred leagues of the British coast; but along the coasts of Africa and South America it is met with periodically, in considerable numbers. In these regions, it is attacked and captured by the southern British and American whalers, as well as by some of the people inhabiting the coasts to which it resorts. Whether this whale is precisely of the same kind as that of Spitzbergen and Greenland is uncertain, though it is evidently a mysticetus. One striking difference, possibly the effect of situation and climate, is, that the mysticetus in southern regions is often covered with barnacles, while those of the Arctic Seas are free from these shell-fish.

Besides the formidable inroads made upon the whale by man, it is subject to annoyance from sharks, and it is also said from the narwal, sword-fish, and thrasher. The opinion as to the narwal I am persuaded is incorrect; the sword-fish and thrasher (if such an animal there be) may be enemies of the whale, and the shark certainly is hostile to the extent of his ability, which, in comparison to that of the whale, can hardly be very formidable.

It is certain that the flesh of the whale is now eaten by savage nations, and it is also well authenticated that, in the twelfth, thirteenth, fourteenth, and fifteenth centuries, it was used as food by the Icelanders, the Netherlander, the French, the Spaniards, and, probably, by the English. Besides forming a choice eatable, the inferior products of the whale are applied to other purposes by the Indians and Esquimaux of Arctic countries, and, with some nations, are essential to their comfort. Some membranes of the abdomen are used for an upper article of clothing, and the peritoneum in particular, being thin and transparent, is used instead of glass in the windows of their huts; the bones are converted into harpoons and spears for striking the seal, or darting at the sea-birds, and are also employed in the erection of their tents, and, with some tribes, in the formation of their boats; the sinews are divided into filaments, and used as thread, with which they join the seams of their boats and tent-cloths, and sew, with great taste and nicety, the different articles of dress they manufacture; and the whalebone and other superior products, so valuable in European markets, have also their uses among them.

The largest animal of the whale tribe is not the mysticetus, but the *Balæna physalis* of Linnæus, *Balænoptera gibbar* of La Cepède, and razor-back of the whalers. This is, probably, the most powerful and bulky of created beings. In comparison with the mysticetus, it has a form less cylindrical, a body longer and more slender, whalebone shorter, produce in blubber and oil less, colour bluer, fins more numerous, breathing more violent, speed greater, and actions quicker, more restless and more bold. Its length is about one hundred feet, and its greatest circumference thirty or thirty-five. Its colour is a pale bluish black, or dark bluish grey, in which it resembles the sucking mysticetus. Besides the two pectoral fins, it has a small horny protuberance, or rayless and immovable fin on the extremity of the back. Its greatest velocity in swimming is about twelve miles an hour. It is by no means a timid animal, yet it does not appear revengeful or mischievous. When closely pursued by boats, it manifests little fear, and does not attempt to outstrip them in the race, but merely endeavours to avoid them by diving or changing its direction. If harpooned, or wounded, it then exerts all its energies, and escapes with its utmost velocity, but shows little disposition to retaliate on its enemies, or to repel their attacks by engaging in a combat. Unlike the mysticetus, it very rarely, when descending into the water, throws its tail into the air. Its great speed and activity render it a difficult and dangerous object of attack, and the small quantity of inferior oil it affords makes it unworthy the general attention of the fishers. When struck, it not uncommonly drags the fast-boat with such speed through the water, that it is liable to be carried immediately beyond the reach of assistance, and soon out of sight of both boats and ship. Hence the striker is under the necessity of cutting the line, and sacrificing his employer's property for securing the safety of himself and his companions. In the year 1818, I ordered a general chase of them, providing against the danger of having my crew separated from the ship by appointing a rendezvous on the shore not far distant, and preparing against the loss of much line by dividing it at two hundred fathoms from the harpoon, and affixing a buoy to the end of it. Thus arranged, one of these whales was shot, and another struck. The former dived with such impetuosity that the line was broken by the resistance of the buoy, as soon as it was thrown into the water, and the latter was liberated within a minute by the division of the line, occasioned, it was supposed, by its friction against the dorsal fin. Both of them escaped. Another physalis was struck by one of my inexperienced harpooners, who mistook it for a mysticetus. It dived obliquely with such velocity that four hundred and eighty fathoms of line were withdrawn from the boat in about a minute of time. This whale was also lost by the breaking of the line.

The physalis occurs in great numbers in the Arctic Seas, especially along the edge of the ice, between Cherie Island and Nova Zembla, and also near Jan Mayen. Persons trading to Archangel have often mistaken it for the common whale. It is seldom seen among much ice, and seems to be avoided by the mysticetus; hence the fishers view it with painful concern. It inhabits most generally in the Spitzbergen quarter the parallels of 70° to 76°; but in the months of June, July, and August, when the sea is usually open, it advances along the land to the northward as high as 80° of latitude. In open seasons it is seen near the headland at an earlier period. A whale, probably of this kind, one hundred and one feet in length, was stranded on the banks of the Humber, about the middle of September, 1750.

Another species of whale frequenting the coasts of Scotland, Ireland, Norway, etc., is the *Balænoptera rorqual* of La Cepède, *Balæna musculus* of Linnæus, or the broad-nosed whale.

In many characters, this species resembles the physalis, though, I think, with an essential difference. The musculus is shorter, having a larger head and mouth, and a rounder under-jaw than the physalis and is said to feed principally upon herrings. Several individuals, apparently of this kind, have been stranded or killed on different parts of the coast of the United Kingdom. One was embayed and killed in Balta Sound, Shetland, in the winter of 1817-18, some remains of which I saw. It was eighty-two feet in length, the jaw-bones were twenty-one feet long, and the largest lamina of whalebone about three feet. Instead of hair at the inner edge, and at the point of each blade of whalebone, it had a fringe of bristly fibres, and it was stiffer, harder, and more horny in its texture than common whalebone. It produced only about five tons of oil, all of it of an inferior quality; some of it viscid and bad. It valued, deducting expenses, no more than £60 sterling. It had the usual sulci about the thorax, and a dorsal fin.

A smaller species of whale is *Balænoptera jubartes* of La Cepède, *Balæna boops* of Linnæus, or the finner of the whale-fishers.

The following is its description:—Length, about forty-six feet; greatest circumference of the body, about twenty feet; dorsal protuberance, or fin, about two feet and a half high; pectoral fins, four or five feet long externally, and scarcely a foot broad; tail, about three feet deep and ten broad; whalebone, about three hundred laminæ on each side, the longest about eighteen inches in length, the under-jaw about fifteen feet long, or one-third of the whole length of the animal; sulci, about two dozen in number; two external blow-holes; blubber on the body two or three inches thick, under the sulci none.

The last, and smallest of the whalebone whales, with which I am acquainted, is the *Balænoptera acuto-rostrata* of La Cepède, *Balæna rostrata* of Linnæus, or the beaked whale. An animal of this kind was killed in Scalpa Bay, November 14,

1808. Its length was seventeen and a half feet, circumference twenty. Pectoral fins, two feet long and seven inches broad; dorsal fin fifteen inches long by four and a half feet broad. Largest whalebone, about six inches. The rostrata is said to inhabit principally the Norwegian Seas, and to grow to the length of twenty-five feet. One of the species was killed near Spitzbergen, in 1813, and I have some of the whalebone in my possession.

Three species of narwals are noticed by La Cepède, though I myself have seen but one, and perhaps the other species are imaginary, for the animal varies in appearance. It is the *Monodon monoceros* of Linnæus, and the narwal, or unicorn, of whalers.

It is, when full grown, from thirteen to sixteen feet in length, exclusive of the tusk; and in circumference (two feet behind the fins, where it is thickest,) eight to nine feet. The form of the head, with the part of the body before the fins, is paraboloidal; of the middle of the body, nearly cylindrical; of the hinder-part, to within two or three feet of tail, somewhat conical, and from thence a ridge, commencing both at the back and belly; the section becomes first an ellipse, and then a rhombus, at the junction of the tail. At the distance of twelve or fourteen inches from the tail the perpendicular diameter is about twelve inches, the transverse diameter about seven. The head is about one-seventh of the whole length of the animal; it is small, blunt, round, and of a paraboloidal form. The mouth is small and not capable of much extension. The under-lip is wedge-shaped. The eyes are small, the largest diameter being only an inch, and are placed in a line with the opening of the mouth about thirteen inches from the snout. The blow-hole, which is directly over the eyes, is a single opening, of a semicircular form, about three and a half inches in diameter, or breadth, and one and a half radius, or length. The fins are twelve or fourteen inches long, and six or eight broad; the tail, from fifteen to twenty inches long, and three to four feet broad. It has no dorsal fin, but in place of it an irregular, sharpish, fatty ridge. The colour of the narwal is in the young animal blackish grey, on the back variegated with numerous darker spots, running into one another; in the older animals the ground is wholly white, or yellowish white. The integuments are similar to those of the mysticetus, only thinner.

A long prominent tusk, with which some narwals are furnished, is considered as a horn by the whale-fishers, and as such has given occasion for the name of *unicorn* being applied to this animal. This tusk occurs on the left side of the head, and is sometimes found of the length of nine or ten feet; according to Egedé, fourteen or fifteen. It springs from the lower part of the upper-jaw, points forward and a little downward, being parallel in its direction to the roof of the mouth. It is spirally situated from right to left, is nearly straight, and tapers to around, blunt point, is of a yellowish white colour, and consists of a compact kind of ivory. It is usually hollow from the base to within a few inches of the point. In a five feet tusk the diameter at the base is two and a quarter inches, and about three-eighths within an inch of the end. This external tusk is peculiar to the male, and there is another imbedded in the skull, on the right side of the head, about nine inches long. Two or three instances have occurred of male narwals having been taken, which had two large external tusks. The use of the tusk is ambiguous. It cannot be essential for procuring their food, nor for defence. Dr. Barclay is of opinion that it is principally a sexual distinction; and it appears not improbable that it is used in piercing the ice for convenience of breathing, without the animal being obliged to retreat to open water. If this latter supposition be correct, it affords another illustration of the wisdom of the great Creator, who has adapted in so many instances the organization of every animal to the locality which it inhabits.

A quantity of blubber, from two to three and a half inches in thickness, and amounting sometimes to above half a ton, encompasses the whole body of the narwal, and affords a large proportion of very fine oil. In a fine fatty substance about the internal ears of the narwal are found multitudes of worms. They are about an inch in length, some shorter, very slender, and taper both ways, but are sharper at one end than at the other. They are transparent. The vertebral column of the narwal is about twelve feet in length. The cervical vertebræ are seven in number, the dorsal twelve, the lumbar and caudal thirty-five. The spinal marrow appears to run through the processes of all the vertebræ from the head to the fortieth, but does not penetrate the forty-first. The ribs are twelve on each side, six true and six false, and are small for the size of the animal. The principal food of the narwal are molluscous animals. I have found remains of sepiæ in several stomachs which I have examined. Narwals are quick, active, inoffensive animals, and swim with considerable velocity. They appear in numerous little herds of half a dozen or more together, each herd being most frequently composed of animals of the same sex. When harpooned, the narwal dives with almost the velocity of the mysticetus, but not to the same extent; on returning to the surface it is dispatched with a lance in a few minutes.

Passing now from these tribes, a short space must be allotted to the description of the dolphins. The first is *Delphinus deductor*, defined by Dr. Traill, the ca'ing or leading whale. The following are its specific characters. Body thick, black; one short dorsal fin; pectoral fins long, narrow; head obtuse; upper jaw bent forward; teeth subconoid, sharp, and a little bent.

This animal grows to the length of about twenty-four feet, and is about ten feet in circumference. The skin is smooth, resembling oiled-silk; the colour a white blueish black on the back, and generally whitish on the belly; the blubber is three or four inches thick. The head is short and round; the upper jaw projects a little over the lower. Externally it has a single spiracle. The full grown have generally twenty-two to twenty-four teeth in each jaw, and when the mouth is shut, the teeth lock between one another like the teeth of a trap. The tail is about five feet broad, the dorsal fin about fifteen inches high, cartilaginous, and immovable.

This kind of dolphin sometimes appears in large herds off the Orkney, Shetland, and Feroe islands. The main body of the herd follows the leading whales, and from this property the animal is called in Shetland the ca'ing whale, and by Dr. Traill the deductor. Many herds of this animal have been driven on shore at different periods, and it is recorded that there were taken in two places in the year 1664 about a thousand; and in modern times extensive slaughters have taken place on the shores of the British and other northern islands.

The *Delphinapterus beluga* of La Cepède, *Delphinus Leucas* of Linnæus, *Beluga* of Pennant, or white whale of the fishers, is the last of the cetacea to which we shall refer. It is not unlike the narwal in its general form, but is thicker about the middle of its body in proportion to its length. Both jaws are furnished with teeth. It has no dorsal fin. The skin is smooth, the colour white. A male animal of this kind was taken in the Frith of Forth in June, 1815. The length was thirteen feet four inches, and the greatest circumference nine feet. The beluga is generally met with in families or herds of five or ten together. They are plentiful in Hudson's Bay, Davis's Strait, and on some parts of the northern coasts of Europe and Asia, where they frequent some of the larger rivers. They are taken for the sake of the oil they produce by harpoons or strong nets; in the latter case, the nets are extended across the stream, so as to prevent their escape out of the river, and when thus interrupted in their course to seaward, they are attacked with lances, and great numbers are sometimes killed.

It is now our purpose to give an account of the *quadrupeds* which inhabit Spitzbergen and the icy seas adjacent.

The connecting link between the mammalia of the land and the water is *Trichecus rosmarus*, walrus, morse, or sea-horse of the whale-fishers. It corresponds in several of its characters both with the bullock and the whale. It grows to the bulk of an ox. Its canine teeth, two in number, are of the length externally of ten to twenty inches, (some naturalists say three feet,) and extend downward from the upper jaw, and include the point of the lower jaw between them. They are incurvated inward. Their full length when cut out of the skull is commonly fifteen to twenty inches, sometimes almost thirty, and their weight five to ten pounds each or upward. The walrus being a slow clumsy animal on land, its tusk seems necessary for its defence against the bear, and also for enabling it to raise its unwieldy body upon the ice when its access to the shore is prevented.

The walrus is found on the shores of Spitzbergen twelve to fifteen feet in length, and eight to ten feet in circumference. The head is short, small, and flattened in front. The flattened part of the face is set with strong bristles. The nostrils are on the upper part of the snout, through which it blows like a whale. The fore paws, which are a kind of webbed hand, are two-sevenths of the full length of the animal from the snout. They are from two to two and a half feet in length, and being expansive maybe stretched to the breadth of fifteen to eighteen inches. The hind feet, which form a sort of tail fin, extend straight backward. They are not united, but detached from each other. The length of each is about two to two and a half feet; the breadth, when fully extended, two and a half or three feet; the termination of each toe is marked by a small tail.

The skin of the walrus is about an inch thick, and it is covered with a short, yellowish brown coloured hair. The inside of the paws in old animals is defended by a rough, horny kind of casing, a quarter of an inch thick, probably produced by the hardening of the skin in consequence of coarse usage in climbing over ice and rocks.

Beneath the skin is a thin layer of fat. At some seasons the produce is said to be considerable, but I have never met with any that afforded above twenty or thirty gallons of oil. In the stomachs of walruses I have met with shrimps, a kind of craw-fish, and the remains of young seals.

It is not at all improbable that the walrus has afforded foundation for some of the stories of mermaids. I have myself seen a sea-horse in such a position, that it requires little stretch of imagination to mistake it for a human being; so like, indeed, was it, that the surgeon of the ship actually reported to me that he had seen a man with his head just appearing above the surface of the water.

The walrus is a fearless animal. It pays no regard to a boat, excepting as an object of curiosity. It is sometimes taken by a harpoon when in the water. If one attack fails, it often affords an opportunity for repeating it. The capture cannot be always accomplished without danger, for, as they go in herds, an attack made upon one individual draws all its companions to its defence. In such cases they frequently rally round the boat from which the blow was struck, pierce its planks with their tusks, and, though resisted in the most determined manner, sometimes raise themselves upon the gunwale, and threaten to overset it. The best defence against these enraged animals is, in such a crisis, sea-sand, which, being thrown into their eyes, occasions a partial blindness, and obliges them to disperse. When on shore they are best killed with long sharp-pointed knives.

The tusks of the walrus, which are hard, white, and compact ivory, are employed by dentists in the fabrication of false teeth. The skin is used in place of mats for defending the yards and rigging of ships from being chafed by friction against each other. When cut into shreds and plaited into cordage, it answers admirably for wheel-ropes, being stronger and wearing much longer than hemp. In ancient times, most of the ropes of ships, in northern countries at least, would appear to have been made of this substance. When tanned, it is converted into a soft porous leather, above an inch in thickness, but it is by no means so useful or so durable as in its green or raw state.

As early as the ninth century, we have accounts of the walrus being extensively fished for on the western coast of Norway. Prior to the institution of the Spitzbergen whale-fishery, the capture of this animal was an object of some commercial importance. It was at first attacked by the English, on Cherie Island, but being driven from thence, if not extirpated in that quarter, by the great slaughter that was carried on, it was then pursued to Spitzbergen. The earliest attacks made on it were very unsuccessful, but experience rendered the assailants more skilful, and, in one voyage, nine hundred or one thousand sea-horses were killed in less than seven hours. The Russians now, rather than the British, are their enemies.

With the exception of the head, the general form of the walrus is similar to the next animal which we describe, the phoca, or seal.

Several species of seals occur in the Greenland Sea, and resort to the ice in the neighbourhood of Spitzbergen and Jan Mayen, in immense herds; but, as the seal frequents the British coast, and is a well-described and well-known animal, I shall not particularize the well-known species that are met with in the Arctic Seas. Some few general observations only will be necessary.

Seals are generally fat in the spring of the year, and afford several gallons of blubber; even small seals will then yield about four or five gallons of oil. The voice of the young seal when in pain or distress is a whining cry, resembling that of a child. They appear to hear well under water; music, or particularly a person whistling, draws them to the surface, and induces them to stretch their necks to the utmost extent, so as to prove a snare by bringing them within reach of the shooter. The most effectual way of shooting them is by the use of small shot, fired into their eyes; when killed with a bullet they generally sink, and are lost. Seals are often seen on their passage from one situation to another in very large shoals. Their general conduct in such cases is such as to amuse spectators, and the sailors call such a shoal a "seal's wedding." The feet of seals are better adapted for motion in the water than on land. They feed on birds, crabs, and small fishes, and are very tenacious of life.

The uses of the seal are various, and to some nations highly important. It yields train-oil, and its skin is extensively employed in making shoes, and, when dressed with the hair, in covering trunks. To the Esquimaux the seal is everything. Its flesh is food, its fat gives light, and its skin, dressed so as to be waterproof, is used for covering for boats and tents, and for garments.

The *Phoca vitulina* is the common species in the Greenland Sea, especially near Jan Mayen. The hooded seal is common near Spitzbergen. The latter is longer than the former, and is said to grow to the length of ten or twelve feet. It is also much more formidable. Seals are not fond of the water, but, when on the ice, are extremely watchful, and secure their retreat either by reclining at the edge or by keeping a hole in the ice open for them. The young ones, however, are not so wary as the old folks. The best situation for the seal-fishery in the Arctic Sea is in the vicinity of Jan Mayen, and the best season March and April. The capture of the seal is the work of a moment. A blow with a seal-club on the nose immediately stuns it, and affords opportunity of making a prize of many at a time. Ships fitted out for the whale-fishery have accidentally obtained in April from two thousand to three thousand seals, and sometimes more; and vessels sent out for seal-fishery only, four thousand or five thousand, yielding nearly one hundred tons of oil. From the ports of the Elbe and Weser a number of sealers are annually dispatched, but few comparatively on this pursuit alone sail from Britain.

Of the dangers of the seal-fishery, arising from the liability to heavy storms at the season and in the place where seals are taken, the following narrative will furnish full illustration.

Fifty-four ships, chiefly Hamburghers, were, in the year 1774, fitted out for seal-fishery alone from foreign ports. In the spring of the year they met with several English ships on the borders of the ice, about sixty miles to the eastward of the island of Jan Mayen. While the boats of the fleet were in search for seals, a dreadful storm suddenly arose. Almost all the people who were at a distance from the ships perished. The Duke of York, captain Peters, had two boats at that time down. The crews of these by great exertion rowed up to the ship, got hold of the rudder rings, but were unable to make their way alongside; they held fast for some time, but the sea was too strong for them, and they lost their hold and fell astern. The chief-mate of the ship, seeing that they were too exhausted to recover their position, determined to attempt their rescue at the peril of his own life. He manned a boat with six stout seamen beside himself, and went to their assistance. On reaching them he exchanged four of his vigorous crew for two of the fainting men in each boat. Thus reinforced, the three boats, by the exertions of their crews, were brought to the stern of the ship; but while in this critical situation, a sea struck the boats, filled and overwhelmed them, on which the whole of their crews, nineteen men, perished. This was only a portion of the disasters of the storm. One ship foundered in a heavy surge, and all hands were lost. Another was wrecked on the ice, and all hands perished. Many boats and men were washed from several others, and the results were that about four hundred foreign seamen, and two hundred British, were drowned, four or five ships lost, and scarcely any escaped without damage.

To all those who navigate the treacherous ocean, especially to such as do business in such dangerous waters, it ought to be of more than ordinary importance to live in a continued preparation for death and judgment, and to be the servants of that God who

"—— rides upon the stormy sky

And manages the seas."

Beneath his care the mariner is safe, and whether from the abysses of its ancient caves, or the foundations of its lofty icebergs, the sea must surrender unto eternal life the bodies of the disciples of Jesus.

The Arctic fox, *Canis lagopus*, is an animal known to those who winter in Spitzbergen, though seldom seen by the whale-fishers. They are rarely found on the ice, though I have often found their impressions on the snow. They are of a white colour, and not easily distinguished.

A more remarkable animal is the Polar or Greenland bear, *Ursus maritimus*. He is the sovereign of the quadrupeds of the Arctic countries. He is powerful and courageous; savage and sagacious; apparently clumsy, yet not inactive. His senses are extremely acute, especially his sight and smell. As he traverses extensive fields of ice, he mounts the hummocks and looks for prey, and on rearing his head and snuffing the breeze, he can perceive the scent of the carrion of the whale at an immense distance. Seals are his usual food, but from their watchfulness he is often obliged to fast. He is as much at home on the ice as on the land, and is found on field-ice above two hundred miles from shore. He can swim with the velocity of three miles an hour, and can dive to a considerable distance.

Bears occur in Spitzbergen, Nova Zembla, Greenland, and other Arctic countries, throughout the year. In some places, they are met with in great numbers. By means of the ice, they often effect a landing on Iceland, but as soon as they appear, they are generally attacked by the inhabitants and destroyed. On the east coast of Greenland, they have appeared like flocks of sheep on a common.

The size of the bear is generally four or five feet in height, seven or eight in length, and nearly as much in circumference. Sometimes, however, the size is much larger. His paws are seven inches in breadth, and his claws two inches in length. His canine teeth, exclusive of the part in the jaw, are about an inch and a half in length. He has been known by the strength of his jaw to bite a lance in two, though made of iron half an inch in diameter. In the water he can be captured without much danger, but on land the experiment is hazardous. When pursued and attacked, he turns upon his enemies. He always, however, unless urged by hunger, retreats before men. His general walk is slow, but upon the ice he can easily outrun any man. If struck with a lance, he is apt to seize it in his mouth, and either bite it in two, or wrest it out of the hand. If shot with a ball, unless he is struck in the head, in the heart, or in the shoulder, he is enraged rather than depressed, and falls with increased power upon his pursuers. When shot at a distance, and able to escape, he has been observed to retire to the shelter of a hummock, and, as if conscious of the styptical effect of cold, apply snow with his paws to the wound.

The bear feeds on the kreng, or carcases of the whales, as they are left by the fishers; on seals, birds, foxes, and deer, when it can surprise them; on eggs, and indeed on any animal substance that comes within its power. The skin of the bear, when dressed with the hair on, forms beautiful mats for a hall or for the bottom of a carriage. Prepared without being ripped up, and the hairy side turned inward, it forms a very warm sack bed, and is used as such in some parts of Greenland. The flesh, when cleared of the fat, is well flavoured and savoury, especially the muscular part of the ham. I once treated my surgeon with a dinner of bears ham, and he did not know for above a month afterwards, but that it was beefsteak. The liver is very unwholesome.

Bears are remarkably affectionate towards their young, and peculiarly sagacious. The female has generally two at a birth. On one occasion, a mother bear with two cubs was pursued across a field of ice by a party of armed sailors. At first, she urged her young ones to increase their speed, but finding the pursuers gaining on them, she carried or pushed or pitched them alternately forward, until she effected their escape. The little creatures are said to have placed themselves across her path to receive her impulse, and when thrown forward they ran on till she overtook them, when they adjusted themselves for a second throw.

Many instances have been observed of the peculiar sagacity of these animals. A seal, lying on the middle of a large piece of ice, with a hole just before it, was marked out by a bear for its prey, and secured by the artifice of diving under the ice, and making its way to the hole by which the seal was prepared to retreat. The seal, however, observed its approach, and plunged into the water, but the bear instantly sprang upon it, and appeared in about a minute afterwards with the seal in its mouth.

The captain of one of the whalers being anxious to procure a bear without wounding the skin, made trial of the stratagem of laying the noose of a rope in the snow, and placing a piece of kreng within it. A bear, ranging the neighbouring ice, was soon enticed to the spot by the smell of burning meat. He perceived the bait, approached, and seized it in his mouth, but his foot, at the same moment, by a jerk of the rope being entangled in the noose, he pushed it off with the adjoining paw, and deliberately retired. After having eaten the piece he carried away with him he returned. The noose, with another piece of kreng, being then replaced, he pushed the rope aside, and again walked triumphantly off with the kreng. A third time the noose was laid, and this time the rope was buried in the snow and the bait laid in a deep hole dug in the centre. But Bruin, after snuffing about the place for a few minutes, scraped the snow away with his paw, threw the rope aside, and escaped unhurt with his prize.

In the month of June, 1812, a female bear, with two cubs, approached the ship I commanded, and was shot. The cubs, not attempting to escape, were taken alive. These animals, though at first evidently very unhappy, became at length, in some measure, reconciled to their situation, and being tolerably tame, were allowed occasionally to go at large about the deck. While the ship was moored to a floe, a few days after they were taken, one of them, having a rope fastened round its neck, was thrown overboard. It immediately swam to the ice, got upon it, and attempted to escape. Finding itself, however, detained by the rope, it endeavoured to disengage itself in the following ingenious way:—Near the edge of the floe was a crack in the ice, of considerable length, but only eighteen inches or two feet wide, and three or four feet deep. To this spot the bear returned; and when, on crossing the chasm, the bight of the rope fell into it, he placed himself across the opening; then, suspending himself by his hind feet, with a leg on each side, he dropped his head and most of his body into the chasm, and, with a foot applied to each side of the neck, attempted for some minutes to push the rope over his head. Finding this scheme ineffectual, he removed to the main ice, and running with great impetuosity from the ship, gave a remarkable pull on the rope; then, going backward a few steps, he repeated the jerk. At length, after repeated attempts to escape this way, every failure of which he announced by a significant growl, he yielded himself to his hard necessity, and lay down on the ice in angry and sullen silence.

Accidents with bears occasionally occur; not so many, however, as the ferocity of these animals, and the temerity of the sailors, might lead one to expect. Some of the early voyagers to the Polar Seas had hard conflicts with them. Barentz's crew especially were often in danger from them, but always succeeded either in conquering or repelling them. Two, however, of the crew of a vessel which had anchored near Nova Zembla, landed on an island at the mouth of the Weigats, and, impelled by curiosity, wandered some distance from the beach; but, whilst unconscious of danger, one of them was suddenly seized on the back by a bear, and brought to the earth. His companion ran off, and gave the alarm, and a party of his shipmates came to their assistance. The bear stood over its prey during their approach without the least appearance of fear and, on their attack, sprang upon one of their number, and made him also a victim to its ferocity and power. The rest now fled in confusion, and could not be induced to renew the conflict. Three sailors only among the crew had sufficient courage to combat with this formidable animal; they attacked it, and, after a dangerous struggle, killed it, and rescued the mangled bodies of their two unfortunate shipmates.

Captain Cook, of the Archangel, of Lynn, being near the coast of Spitzbergen, in the year 1788, landed, accompanied by his surgeon and mate. While traversing the shore, the captain was unexpectedly attacked by a bear, which seized him in an instant between its paws. At this awful juncture, when a moment's pause must have been fatal to him, he called to his surgeon to fire; who, with admirable resolution and steadiness, discharged his piece as directed, and providentially shot the bear through the head. The captain, by this prompt assistance, was preserved from being torn to pieces.

On a more recent occasion, a commander of a whale ship was in a similar danger. Captain Hawkins, of the Everthorpe, of Hull, when in Davis's Strait, in July, 1818, seeing a very large bear, took a boat, and pushed off in pursuit of it. On reaching it, the captain struck it twice with a lance in the breast; and, while in the act of recovering his weapon for another blow, the enraged animal sprang up, and seized him by the thigh, and threw him over its head into the water. Fortunately it did not repeat its attack, but exerted itself to escape. This exertion, when the attention of every one was directed towards their captain, was not made in vain, for it was allowed to swim away without further molestation.

With regard to curious adventures, on one occasion a bear, which was attacked by a boat's crew, made such formidable resistance, that it was enabled to climb the side of the boat and take possession of it, while the intimidated crew fled for safety to the water, supporting themselves by the gunwale and rings of the boat, until, by the assistance of another party from the ship it was shot, as it sat inoffensively in the stern. With regard to narrow escapes, a sailor, who was pursued on a field of ice by a bear, when at a considerable distance from assistance, preserved his life by throwing down an article of clothing whenever the bear gained upon him, on which it always suspended the pursuit until it had examined it, and thus gave him time to obtain some advance. In this way, by means of a hat, a jacket, and a neckerchief, successively cast down, the progress of the bear was retarded, and the sailor escaped from the danger that threatened him, in the refuge afforded him by his vessel.

The rein-deer, *Cervus tarandus*, deserves to be mentioned amongst the quadrupeds of the Arctic regions. I have never seen one myself, though it is known to inhabit almost every part of Spitzbergen.

Our remarks must now be directed to the *Birds* which frequent the sea and coast of Spitzbergen.

The brent goose and eider duck, *Anas bernicla* and *Anas mollissima*, are found in these regions; the former occurring in considerable numbers near the coast of Greenland, but not in Spitzbergen, and the latter frequenting all the islands in the Greenland Sea. The puffin, or Greenland parrot, *Alca arctica*, feeding on shrimps, is rarely seen out of sight of land, but is very common near the coast of Spitzbergen. *Alca alle*, also, the little auk or roach, is an extremely numerous species in some situations in the Polar Seas. They occur in the water in thousands together, and sometimes in like abundance on the pieces of ice. They dive quickly on being alarmed, and on the approach of thick weather they are particularly noisy.

The fulmar, *Procellaria glacialis*, is the constant companion of the whale-fisher. It joins his ship immediately on passing the Shetland Islands, and accompanies it through the trackless ocean to the highest accessible latitudes. It keeps an eager watch for anything thrown overboard; the smallest particle of fatty substance can scarcely escape it. As such, a hook baited with a piece of fat meat or blubber, and towed by a long twine over the ship's stern, is a means employed by the sailor-boys for taking them. In the spring of the year, before they have glutted themselves with the fat of the whale, they are pretty good eating. They are remarkably easy and swift on the wing, and can fly to windward in the highest storms. Though very few fulmars should be seen when a whale is about being captured, yet, as soon as the flensing commences, they rush in from all quarters, and seize, with great audacity, all the pieces of fat that come in their way. They frequently glut themselves so completely as to be unable to fly, in which case, when not relieved by a quantity being disgorged, they rest on the ice until restored by digestion. The fulmar is a bold and very hardy bird. Its feathers being thick, it is not easily killed with a blow. Its bite, from the crookedness, strength, and sharpness of its bill, is very severe. Fulmars differ in colour; some are a dirty grey, others much paler, and totally white on the breast and belly. In size this bird is a little smaller than a duck. Beneath its feathers is a thick bed of fine grey down. When carrion is scarce, the fulmar sometimes points out the whale to the fisher by following in its track. They cannot make much impression on the dead whale until some more powerful animal tears away the skin.

The tysté, or doveca, *Colymbus grylle*, is a beautifully formed bird, occurring in considerable numbers in icy situations, at various distances from land. It is so watchful, and so quick at diving, that, if fired at without precaution to conceal the flash of the powder, it generally escapes the shot. It feeds on shrimps and small fishes. The common colour is black, but the feet are all red.

Almost equally common with the preceding is the *Colymbus troile*, a clumsy bird, weighing two pounds or upwards, and measuring only sixteen or seventeen inches in length, and twenty-eight inches across the wings, when full spread, in breadth. It cannot rise on the wing in any direction except to windward. If it attempts to fly to leeward, it runs for a considerable distance along the surface of the water, and at length falls into it. Both in this instance and that of the doveca, shortness of tail is compensated for by the feet, which are used as a rudder in flying. The *Colymbus glacialis* was seen by captain Phipps on the coast of Spitzbergen.

The sea-swallow, or great tern, *Sterna hirundo*, is an elegant bird, common on the shore of Spitzbergen, but is not met with at a distance from land. Its length is seven or eight inches, and including the tail fourteen, and the spread of its wings twenty-nine or thirty inches. It flies with great ease and swiftness, and to a considerable height. It defends its eggs and young with great boldness from the Arctic gull, and even descends within a yard of the head of any person who ventures to molest them, startling him with its loud screams. It lays its eggs among the shingle of the beach above high-water mark, where the full power of the sun falls.

There are several varieties of the gull tribe. The kittywake, *Larus rissa*, is seen in every part of the northern Atlantic from Britain to the highest latitudes. It is a better fisher than its enemy, the Arctic gull, *Larus parasiticus*, by whom it is pursued until it gives up the food it has procured. The latter kind of gull lives at the expense of its neighbours, preying upon their eggs and their young. *Larus crepidatus* and *Larus eburneus* are other varieties. The latter, remarkable for its immaculate whiteness, is as ravenous as the fulmar. *Larus glaucus*, burgomaster, is the chief magistrate of the feathered tribe in the Spitzbergen regions, as none of its class dare dispute its authority, or refuse at its bidding to surrender their prey. It is a large and powerful bird, twenty-eight inches in length, and five inches in breadth across the wings. The kittywake, snow-bird, and burgomaster, are sometimes shot for the sake of their feathers. The two latter species are very shy. They are shot with the greatest ease, however, from a house built of snow on the ice. The *Tringa hypoleucos*, sandpiper, and the *Emberiza nivalis*, snow-bunting, are inhabitants also of these regions. A bird of great delicacy and smallness is *Fringilla linaria*, the lesser redpole. On our approach to Spitzbergen, several of this species alighted on the ship, and were, apparently, so wearied by flight that they allowed themselves to be taken alive. It is difficult to understand how this small bird manages to perform the journey from Spitzbergen to a milder climate, without becoming exhausted and perishing by the way.

The *Amphibia, Fishes, Animalcules*, etc., must conclude our sketch of the zoology of the Arctic regions.

In the class *Amphibia*, the most notable personage is the Greenland shark, *Squalus borealis*. It has not, I believe, been described. The ventral fins are separate. It is without anal fin, but has the temporal opening, and it belongs, therefore, to the third division of the genus. The spiracles on the neck are five in number on each side. The colour is cinereous grey. The eyes are the most extraordinary part of the animal. The pupil is emerald green, the rest of the eye blue. To the posterior edge of the pupil is attached a white vermiform substance, one or two inches in length. Each extremity of it consists of two filaments, but the central part is single. The sailors imagine this shark is blind, because it pays not the least attention to the presence of a man, and is, indeed, so apparently stupid, that it never draws back when a blow is aimed at it with a knife or a lance. It is twelve or fourteen feet in length, and six or eight feet in circumference, and in general form very much resembles the dog-fish. It is one of the foes of the whale. It bites and annoys it when living, and feeds on it when dead. With its teeth, which are serrated in one jaw, and lancet-shaped and denticulated in the other, it scoops out of the body of the whale pieces as large as a person's head, and continues scooping and gorging till its belly is filled. It is so insensible to pain that, though run through the body with a knife, it will return to its food, and for some hours after its heart is taken out, or its body cut in pieces, they will continue to show signs of life. It does not, so far as I am aware, attack the fishers.

In the class *Pisces*, *Gadus carbonarius*, the coal-fish, was procured by captain Phipps, as also of the former class, *Cyclopterus liparis*, during his stay in the vicinity of Spitzbergen. *Mullus barbatus* was taken out of the mouth of a seal by a seaman, near Spitzbergen. It was boiled by our officers, and proved an excellent dish.

In the class *Articulata* are one or two species of *gammarus*. The *G. arcticus* of Leach, the actions of which suggest as a familiar name, the mountebank shrimp. There are also various crabs, and the *Oniscus ceti* of Linnæus, or whale's louse. This little animal is about half an inch in diameter, and firmly fixes itself by hooked claws on the skin of the mysticetus. It is found under the fin, and wherever the skin is tender, and it is not likely to be dislodged. A similar animal, though smaller, is found on the body of the narwal.

In the class *Vermes* are several species found in various animals inhabiting the northern seas. The sea-snail, *Clio helicina*, is an animal covered with a delicately beautiful sheet, similar to that of the nautilus. The diameter is from two-eighths to three-eighths of an inch. It is found in great quantities near the coast of Spitzbergen. The *Clio borealis* occurs in vast numbers in some situations near Spitzbergen, but is not found generally in the Arctic Seas. In swimming, it brings the tips of its fins almost into contact, first oil one side and then on another. I kept several of them alive in a glass of sea-water for about, a month, when they gradually wasted away and died.

The cuttle-fish, *Sepia*, were found by me in large numbers in the stomachs of the narwals.

More than six or seven kinds of *Medusæ* may be distinguished, among which may be named, *Medusa pileus*, and the purse-shaped, bottle-shaped, and orange-coloured *medusæ*. *Medusa pileus* is one of the most curious of the tribe. It consists of eight lobes, with a beautiful, irridescent, finny fringe on the external edge of each. A canal, four-fifths the length of the animal, penetrates the centre of it, and two red cirrhi, which may be extended to the length of nearly a foot, proceed from a crooked cavity in opposite sides. The animal is semi-transparent, the colour white, and the finny fringes of deeper red. It is found of various sizes.

The substance of the purse-shaped medusa is tougher than that of any other species which I have examined. It has one large open cavity, and is divided by the finny fringes into eight segments, each alternate pair of which are similar. The colour is a pale crimson, with waved purple lines, and the finny fringes deeper crimson. The animal appeared to be almost without sensation. The only evidence it gave of feeling was in an increased vibration of the finny fringes. Though it was cut into pieces, each portion on which there was any of the fringe continued, by its incessant play, to give evidence of life during two or three days, after which it became putrescent, and began to waste away. I have only seen one specimen of this and of the orange-coloured medusa. The colour of the latter was a brilliant orange, and it was not transparent. It was not tenacious of life, having died, to appearance, soon after it was taken.

The Greenland Sea, frozen and extensive as it is, teems with life. The variety of the animal creation is not, indeed, very great, but the quantity of some of the species that occur is truly immense. The minute medusæ and animalcules, throughout the Spitzbergen Sea, would exceed all the powers of the mind to conceive. These little creatures constitute the food of the largest animals in the creation. The common whale feeds on medusæ, sepiæ, cancri, actiniæ, etc., and these feed, probably, on the minor medusæ animalcules. The finwhales and dolphins feed principally on herrings and other small fishes. These subsist on the smaller cancri, medusæ, and animalcules. The bear's most general food is the seal; the seal subsists on the cancri and small fishes, and these on lesser animals of the tribe, or on the minor medusæ and animalcules. Thus the whole of the larger animals depend on these minute beings, which, until the year 1816, when I first entered on the examination of the sea-water, were not, I believe, known to exist in the Polar Seas.

The manner in which these minute animals are preserved, in a sea which is surrounded by an atmosphere ten or twelve degrees in mean temperature below the freezing point of salt water, is curious and interesting, and illustrates the combined wisdom and goodness of the Lawgiver of these icy regions, as well as of the entire globe. If the water of the sea were stationary, the temperature of the atmosphere would soon freeze it to the very bottom, and destroy all these minute animals, who have not either instinct or power of motion to retire into a more southern region. A current, however, is provided, setting towards the south-west, which carries away the ice into a parallel where it can be dissolved, and creates a circulation of water into the frozen regions from a warmer climate; while therefore the superficial current is carrying away the ice, an under-current, in a contrary direction, is bringing in warmth beneath. But how, it may be asked, does it happen that the minor medusæ are not carried away into the southern region? It is no violation of commonly received principles to suppose, that whenever the medusæ are carried to some extent southward, they sink in the water until they reach the stream of the under-current, and are by it conveyed to their proper element. The fact that the olive-green water of the sea maintains a similar position for years together, while surface after surface of ice is carried away and dissipated, is in support of this conjecture. Thus, by a most beautiful contrivance, a large portion of the surface of the globe is rendered habitable, which would otherwise be a solid mass of ice, and the Polar Sea affords a dwelling-place for many tribes of animals most useful in supplying the wants, and contributing to the comfort, of man.

It is not only, therefore, in those regions where

"Spices breathe and milder seasons smile,"

but even in the laws of a less genial climate, that we are called upon to observe His eternal power and godhead, who gives the bounties of his providence to the just and the unjust, and pleads with us, in the gospel of his Son, that we should be reconciled to him. The mighty whale, the ephemeral insect, and the minute animalcule, all the productions of his power and skill, have their wants supplied by his laws, and are subject to his control. In these he displays the strength of his arm, and the adaptations of his wisdom, but in man, redeemed and sanctified, "the exceeding riches of his grace." Happy, indeed, are we, if whilst, with the ancient psalmist, we can proclaim that the earth is full of the goodness of the Lord, "who gathereth the waters of the sea together as an heap," and "layeth up the depth in store-houses," we can also, without presumption, through our union with the great heir of all things, the

Lord Jesus, and by the merit of his life and death, honestly declare all things are ours, whether ... the world, or life, or death, or things present, or things to come, all are ours, and we are Christ's, and Christ is God's.

CHAPTER VI.

EXPEDITIONS FOR FURTHER DISCOVERY.

Having now completed the account of the Arctic Regions, as given by captain Scoresby, it may be interesting to the reader to have a brief statement of some of the principal expeditions for further discovery down to the present time.

In 1819, lieutenant Parry sailed with the Hecla and Griper. The object of his expedition was to examine the great and open bay, known as sir J. Lancaster's Sound; and, in case of failure, the Sound of alderman Jones, and that of sir T. Smith. On the 1st of August, the ships entered the Sound of sir J. Lancaster, and ran quickly up it, finding no land across the bottom of the inlet, but arriving at a strait, which they named Barrow's Strait, and a magnificent opening into which it led, Wellington Channel. On the 4th of September, the expedition crossed the meridian of 110° west longitude, in latitude 74° 44', becoming entitled to a reward of £5,000. They anchored, and put into winter-quarters at Melville Island, losing sight of the sun from 11th November till the 3rd of February, when it became once more visible from the Hecla's main-top. With the greatest difficulty, they managed to escape from the ice during the months of August and September, arriving at the Orkneys 28th October, 1820.

The second voyage of Parry was with the Fury and Hecla. His instructions were to proceed towards, or into, Hudson's Strait, to penetrate to the westward through that strait, until he should reach some portion of the coast of the continent of America. The object was to discover a way westward from the Atlantic into the Pacific Ocean. The vessels left the Nore 8th May, 1821, and arrived at Resolution Island, at the entrance of Hudson's Strait, on 2nd July, attempted the direct passage through the Frozen Strait, and passed through it into Repulse Bay. From it no passage was found to the west, and the ships, after beating about to no profit, were compelled to winter near Lyon's Inlet. Here the dreariness of the winter was relieved by interviews with the inhabitants, who were found to be intelligent and honest. On 2nd July, the ships left their winter-quarters, and, after being exposed to the most fearful dangers, arrived at a strait, called by Parry, the Strait of the Fury and Hecla, and believed by him to be an opening into the Polar Sea. The ships again went into winter-quarters, and were frozen in until late in the following year, but arrived at Lerwick on October 10th, 1823.

The same ships, under the same commander, sailed on a third expedition in May, 1824, having for its object to penetrate through Lancaster Sound, Barrow's Strait, and Prince Regent's Inlet, to the westward. Through detention by the ice, they did not arrive at Lancaster Sound till 10th September, and went into winter-quarters on the 27th, in Prince Regent's

Inlet, at Port Bowen. On the breaking up of the ice, they explored, southerly, close to the westward shore; but by the accidents to which they were exposed, they were compelled to abandon the Fury, with her stores, and the Hecla only returned to England.

In 1827, captain Parry proposed to reach the North Pole by means of travelling with sledge-boats over the ice. Two boats were constructed for the purpose, the one to be commanded by Parry, the other by lieutenant Ross. They proceeded in the Hecla to Spitzbergen, and there left the ship, starting in their sledge-boats with seventy-one days' provisions. They travelled by night rather than by day; found the ice very rough, and in some places tender; and after experiencing great difficulties, arrived only at latitude 82° 45', and were compelled to abandon the undertaking as hopeless.

Captain John Franklin received instructions to explore the northern coast of America, from the mouth of Copper Mine River to the eastward. He sailed on 22nd May, 1819, in a ship of the Hudson's Bay Company. They arrived at York Factory, in Hudson's Bay, on 30th August. Their route was to be by Cumberland House, and through a chain of posts to the Great Slave Lake. At Cumberland House, it was arranged that Franklin and others should proceed at once on to the Athobasca department, to the northward of the Great Slave Lake, and that the rest of the party should follow in the spring. The place of meeting was Fort Chepewyan, eight hundred and fifty-seven miles from Cumberland House; and, by the 20th August, they had advanced to Fort Enterprise, five hundred and fifty miles from Chepewyan. Here they wintered, and were exposed to awful hardships; but, on the arrival of the spring, they prosecuted their journey down the Copper Mine River, reaching the Polar Sea on the 18th July. They then navigated the coast to the eastward, in their canoes, exploring Coronation Gulf. They attempted to return by Hood's River, and across the land to Point Lake. After being exposed to the most dreadful sufferings, they regained their winter-stations, at Fort Enterprise, and returned to England.

Notwithstanding the perils and hardships which had already befallen them, captain Franklin and his companions, Dr. Richardson and lieutenant Back, undertook a second expedition over the same country, and left Liverpool 16th February, 1825, arriving at Fort Chepewyan as early as 15th July. They then descended Mackenzie River to the sea. Dividing themselves into two parties, they explored the coast east and west, and the expedition returned home 24th September, 1827.

Other voyages are those of Ross, of Back, first and second, and of Dease and Simpson, two officers of the Hudson's Bay Company, who surveyed, in 1839, the remainder of the western coast which had been left by Franklin. Dr. John Rae was dispatched by the Hudson's Bay Company in July, 1846, to survey the unexplored portion of the Arctic coast at the north-eastern angle of the American continent, and returned successfully in October, 1847.

An important expedition for discovery in the North Polar regions, the termination of which is yet awaited with serious anxiety, left England under sir John Franklin in July, 1845. The ships were victualled for only three full years, which expired during the summer of this year. Three expeditions have been sent in search of the lost travellers. One departed early in February, 1848, for Behring's Strait; a second, which sailed in the spring, under sir J. Ross, has been heard of as having reached Disco Island on the 2nd July; and a third, under sir John Richardson, accompanied by Dr. Rae, left in March to proceed overland, and arrived at Lake Superior on 29th of April. A report has very recently come in from the Esquimaux of their having seen "two large boats, full of white men, to the east of the Mackenzie river;" and sir J. Ross has been spoken with by a whaler on the east side of Baffin's Bay, in latitude 74° 20'; but no tidings to relieve the public anxiety have been received to the close of 1848, concerning the fate of sir J. Franklin and his companions.

THE RELIGIOUS TRACT SOCIETY: INSTITUTED 1799